RESTORATIVE JUSTICE

The way ahead

Authors: Shari Tickell and Kate Akester

JUSTICE – advancing justice, human rights and the rule of law

JUSTICE is an independent law reform and human rights organisation. It works largely through policy-orientated research; interventions in court proceedings; education and training; briefings, lobbying and policy advice. It is the British section of the International Commission of Jurists (ICJ).

JUSTICE relies heavily on the help of its members and supporters for the funds to carry out its work. For more information visit www.justice.org.uk.

JUSTICE, 59 Carter Lane, London EC4V 5AQ
Tel: +44 (0)20 7329 5100
Fax: +44 (0)20 7329 5055
E-mail: admin@justice.org.uk
www.justice.org.uk

Designed by Adkins Design
Printed by Fretwells Ltd

Contents

Foreword

Restorative justice is a growth area. After years of struggling to establish itself, it has - with significant international support - definitively arrived. It is now, since the implementation of the Youth Justice and Criminal Evidence Act 1999, an integral part of our youth justice system. I remember how the parliamentary debates at that time made it clear that the government had seen that it was necessary to try and shift thinking in a system that had become beleaguered by criticism.

Now we are going still further. Restorative justice is to be incorporated into the whole criminal justice system: and therefore will be used with adults, in response to serious offences, and possibly even for those difficult and intractable cases involving domestic violence, race hate, and homophobia. This is a momentous change, and developments are accelerating fast.

That is why I am particularly pleased to introduce this report. It is a timely contribution to events. Many people will still be unsure of what restorative justice is. They will find a discussion about the difficulties of defining it; and an explanation of the core principles, and of how they are applied through the various methods of conferencing, mediation, sentencing circles, and victim empathy. This is a useful summary at a time of potentially huge expansion: and it incorporates an up-to-date critique of the advantages and disadvantages of restorative practice, with a plea for it to be used carefully and appropriately.

I share JUSTICE's concern for human rights; and the salutary reminder that the new informal processes may be short on safeguards, depending on participation and organisation, is well put. The role of lawyers is so far the main area of debate; but the questions of accountability and standards are raised too, and these are the subjects of national and international work in progress.

The main body of the report deals with international experience of restorative justice, and it is just what is needed. The decision not to analyse this material in too much detail in favour of giving us a wide-ranging overview of restorative practice in selected jurisdictions around the world is apposite. Beginning with New Zealand and Australia: whose statutory schemes have been the most influential model, we are guided through contrasting, and differently structured initiatives, each with their own history, priorities, and learning points.

The skilled work done on death row in Texas makes compelling reading; and I commended the review of domestic violence and mediation, piloted in Austria amidst considerable controversy. All the examples used give us valuable insights into the way restorative practice might best be organised in this country. This is a constructive contribution, at a time when we must concentrate on implementation, and the practical questions it presents.

JUSTICE does well to remind us of the shortcomings of our current system, and the imperative of improvement; but stresses that this must be done realistically and sensitively - otherwise restorative justice (like many other criminal justice "reforms") will soon be perceived as failing - and will run the risk of being discarded before its potential has been realised.

Despite the recent arrival of the restorative idea, and the challenge we face in building it into our system, it is still necessary to look ahead. JUSTICE finishes by suggesting that we could learn a great deal from tackling the thorny issues, including domestic violence, I have already mentioned. In developing and refining the specialist techniques and training that these will require, we will gain knowledge of how to approach more everyday cases too.

Cherie Booth QC

Introduction

Restorative justice is an idea which has captured imaginations around the world, as this book demonstrates. Its concept has percolated deeply into our youth justice system and is now seeping into the treatment of adults. Both the Court of Appeal and the Lord Chief Justice (as we note at the beginning of chapter 3) have recognised the relevance in sentencing terms of how an offender has coped with mediation with a victim or some other restorative justice intervention.

There is enormous scope for the concepts of restorative justice to deal with the causes of crime in the sense of changing the behaviour of those truly accepting that they have committed crimes; offended society; harmed victims. The first three chapters of this book deal with general issues relating to restorative justice within the wider criminal justice system. Chapters 4-6 cover developments in other relevant jurisdictions – Australia and New Zealand, so important as the sources of experiment with restorative justice; the United States, a profuse source of diverse experiment particularly in the contrasting states of Texas and Minnesota; Austria and Norway, both of whom institutionalise a restorative approach into their criminal justice system. Chapter 7 covers developments in Northern Ireland and Scotland. Chapters 8 and 9 deal with recent developments in England and Wales, respectively with children and adults. Chapter 10 sets out ten lessons that can be drawn from our inquiry.

Much of the fieldwork on this project was undertaken by Shari Tickell. Appendix 3 lists most of the visits and interviews that she undertook. JUSTICE is immensely grateful for her work and that of its former director of criminal justice policy, Kate Akester, who worked with her on the final text. Thanks must go to everyone who assisted in the project and particularly those who, in person or electronically, participated in the review panel that supported the work. This was chaired by Professor Andrew Ashworth QC and included Kathleen Daly, Jim Dignan, Roger Graef, Tapio Lappis-Seppala, Rob Mackay, Gabrielle Maxwell, David Miers, Christa Pelikan, Sir Charles Pollard, Annie Roberts, Caroline Rowe, Debora Singer, Mike Thomas, Barbara Tudor and Dan van Ness. A special mention should be made of Rob Allen, representative of the Esmee Fairbairn Foundation, which funded the research as part of its Rethinking Crime and Punishment initiative and to which we express our considerable gratitude. Rob gave immense assistance to the work.

Executive summary

The criminal justice context (chapter 1)

The government is to be commended for the aim of 'max[imising] the use of restorative justice' set out in its strategy document *Restorative Justice: the government's strategy,* published in July 2003. This commitment must be reflected in its overall criminal justice policy and can play a valuable role in informing credible and constructive alternatives to imprisonment.

Definitions, models and principles (chapter 2)

'Restorative justice' is difficult to define. At its core is a commitment to the idea that victim, offender and the community need to repair the damage caused by the offence through dialogue and negotiation, direct or indirect.

Practice can take many forms but restorative methods share an informal, creative, problem-solving approach, to allow for individually appropriate outcomes. In such schemes, it follows that there needs to be protection for all parties from possible abuse. National standards are required. Victims must not be 're-victimised'. Offenders must not be unduly humiliated.

Human rights and accountability (chapter 3)

International human rights conventions have significantly influenced the spread of restorative justice. Many youth justice systems are based on the ideas and principles we find in them and these are now being applied to adults.

The Human Rights Act 1998 provides an essential framework for developments. We discuss the implications of the relevant articles of the European Convention on Human Rights and case-law requiring that young people are able to participate effectively in these processes, and the obligation to supply legal representation in cases where this cannot be achieved.

A variety of EU and UN guidelines encourage the use of restorative justice and have set out standards for its operation.

Restorative Justice in origin: New Zealand and Australia (chapter 4)

New Zealand made a radical break with the past by introducing family group conferences, now used all over the world, in order to deal with Maori demands for community-based, culturally appropriate solutions to offending. Detention centres were closed and responses to offending de-professionalised. Victims' views had to be explicitly taken into account for the first time, by virtue of the groundbreaking Children, Young Persons and their Families Act 1989.

These ideas were critiqued by a number of jurisdictions in Australia, where practice inspired the use of restorative methods in the UK by the Thames Valley Police.

Restorative Justice in profusion: The United States (chapter 5)

The US provides a wide variety of examples of how restorative justice may be used. For this project, we looked particularly at developments in Minnesota and Texas. The first was characterised by well-developed integration into the system and the latter was particularly interesting because of work done with those in prison, often on death row, for serious crimes.

Restorative Justice in institutionalised settings: Austria and Norway (chapter 6)

These countries provide examples of the use of mediation, thoroughly integrated into the criminal justice system in Austria, and with a wider range of applications and greater community involvement in Norway.

Restorative Justice in Northern Ireland and Scotland (chapter 7)

Restorative justice was developed as part of a grassroots, cross-community desire to lessen violence in Northern Ireland. It has been particularly successful in providing an alternative to punishment violence as a response to crime and antisocial behaviour and has recently made a radical move to introduce mainstream family group conferencing for young people – the first in a UK context. In Scotland, the Scottish Association for the Care and Resettlement of Offenders has built on the non-punitive philosophy and flexible approach of the Children's Hearings and has introduced restorative practice for adults.

Youth justice in England and Wales (chapter 8)

Restorative justice has been introduced as a core element of the arrangements for dealing with young offenders. Our research indicates that this has been generally successful and referral orders now account for one-third of all orders made by youth courts. The government was correct to accept early criticism and make referral orders discretionary in August 2003.

Non-statutory provision: adults and the police in England and Wales (chapter 9)

There are a significant number of different restorative schemes in England and Wales, which are operated by the probation service and others. Thames Valley Police have championed the use of restorative methods and we discuss their role and its future.

Conclusions and the way forward (chapter 10)

To advance restorative justice in the UK, restorative justice should be:

1. regarded, fundamentally, as a set of values rather than one particular model of provision;
2. a framework within which the criminal justice system can move away from over-reliance on punitive imprisonment;
3. realistic and responsive;
4. adequately resourced, so that the support and interventions needed by participants are available;
5. designed to avoid 'net widening', so that minor offenders are not swept into programmes unnecessarily;
6. consistent with the principles of human rights;
7. supported by the development of standards for practice and accountability;
8. conducted by independent practitioners;
9. led by a single body to oversee its development;
10. championed by government.

Chapter 1 – The criminal justice context

This publication takes up the challenge, as did the government itself, of exploring one of the recommendations of Lord Justice Auld's *Review of the Criminal Courts*.[1] He called for:

> *The development and implementation of a national strategy to ensure consistent, appropriate and effective use of restorative justice techniques across England and Wales.*[2]

In arguing for this, Lord Justice Auld acknowledged that he had been influenced by champions of restorative justice in the criminal justice system, such as Sir Charles Pollard, then the chief constable of Thames Valley Police. This is an important consideration. One of the main drivers of reform is the passionate belief of restorative justice practitioners that they have a major contribution to make in serving victims', as well as offenders' needs; and enlightening a criminal justice system, which has, otherwise, become somewhat stuck in processes, procedures and punishment. Restorative justice, very much like alternative dispute resolution (a close relative within the civil justice system), attracts many very remarkable pioneers who are dedicated to, and inspired by, what began as a cause. We met many of them in every country that we visited to research this report.

Lord Justice Auld was similarly impressed:
- He noted that restorative justice: 'has been described as more of a philosophy than a specific model';
- He accepted that it 'embraces diversion in many forms at different stages of the criminal process';
- He recognised the advantages of restorative justice techniques at six stages of the criminal process from before charge to after sentence;
- He called for restorative justice to be put 'under the oversight or direction of a single agency or joint body';
- He observed that 'restorative justice in the short-term is expensive in the range and level of resources necessary to give it a chance of success';
- He required that the courts and the judiciary were given a key role in overseeing the use of restorative justice, emphasising 'the goal of fair and proportionate outcomes'; and

- He noted that 'care will also need to be taken to inform and persuade the public that it is a force for good, in particular, in crime prevention'.

The government promised a response to the Auld review and delivered it in July 2003.[3] This reported on the wide range of restorative justice activities taking place in England and Wales and expressed the government's satisfaction with the same. It stated its aim as being 'to maximise the use of restorative justice ... where we know it works well, to meet victims' needs and to reduce re-offending'.[4] The government announced a two-pronged strategy:

1. 'building in high quality restorative justice at all stages of the criminal justice system' by way of a range of measures including:
   – statutory backing for 'restorative cautioning';
   – piloting programmes for diversion from prosecution;
   – making reparation a statutory purpose of sentencing;
   – setting out action plans for the Prison and Probation Services;
   – incorporating restorative justice into new initiatives for adults, such as intermittent custody orders;
   – 'increasing understanding of restorative justice among professionals and the general public';
   – developing training, practice and accreditation.

2. further research and policy development.

The authors commend the government for much of the thinking in its strategy paper. It is clear that we are now in a period of change, which is potentially mould-breaking. Restorative justice represents a shift in language and orientation, creating an opportunity to reinvigorate debate in a political environment that is explicitly trying to address the causes of crime, rather than responding to the demand for 'toughness' and punishment. What it offers is inclusion for victims and a determined approach to targeting the causes of crime that can, for the offender, be as 'tough' as any conventional criminal justice response, and may be more effective in the longer term. Considering the current climate of dissatisfaction with the existing system, these are prizes worth winning. The government, consulting on these ideas in its strategy document, defines 'restorative justice' as follows:

> *Restorative justice brings victims and offenders into contact, so that victims can get answers to questions, tell the offender what the real impact of their offending was and receive an apology. Restorative justice*

gives offenders the chance to make amends for their crime, either to
victims themselves, or to the community. But restorative justice is about
more than material reparation – it can repair relationships and trust that
have been broken by crime.[5]

Already, this reflects the lessons of experience. Both victims and offenders wishing to participate in restorative justice processes can gain enormously, and have done so in programmes in this country and abroad. The government prefaces its strategy paper with a quotation from an offender who said of a restorative justice conference:

The main lesson I learnt about myself was that my crime affected
everybody concerned – it became more like ten crimes because of all the
people it affected.

Restorative justice, therefore, may offer more to victims than it has been possible to achieve in an adversarial context. The current government's policy is receptive to this and it is now keen to use restorative justice to bring a genuine victim focus into the system. The definitions and nature of restorative justice are considered further in chapter 2. The remainder of this chapter will review some of the difficulties that need to be faced.

The criminological background

The victims' lobby is relatively young. Inevitably, we know much more about offenders. The ineffectiveness of the current system in reducing recidivism and promoting rehabilitation – particularly through lengthening prison sentences – is well documented. Offenders, and society's failure to deal satisfactory with them, have traditionally attracted the most attention. Such new arrangements as there are draw on existing knowledge about offenders: we still lack information about victims and about how restorative methods affect people.[6] This picture will change as collectively we gather experience. Future research will no doubt, be shaped both by the wider social justice perspective required by restorative justice practice and by social inclusion policies.

In the meantime, it is instructive to review what we do know in terms of the criminological background and the current situation. First, we recognise that confidence in the criminal justice system is low – caused by the cumulative effect of a sharp increase in crime rates during the 1960s and 1970s, together with low detection rates and victim dissatisfaction. Higher crime rates allowed crime to be regarded and presented as normal, pervasive and not confined to the margins of society. Criminologist David Garland has written influentially on the subject.[7] He argues that the perceived simultaneous failure of 'penal welfare' approaches towards offenders, and of the system as a whole to deliver a feeling of security, encouraged governments to forge new strategies. Attitudes shifted towards prevention, enhanced control and 'expressive' punishment. The latter has become known as 'punitive segregation' – the removal of offenders from society for long periods of time.

This is done in the name of victims but at the expense of reflecting on the causes of crime. It has come to dominate much contemporary thinking, the prevailing political response to crime, and the public mood. It has fostered the rising prison numbers and longer sentences that have been manifest in both Labour and Conservative administrations and undermined the bold attempt of the Criminal Justice Act 1991 to reach a more rational and humane approach. The influence of policies in the US has also played a significant role. The drive for mandatory sentences – an approach entirely founded on the crime not the criminal – is all part of this approach.

Crime tends to be publicised dramatically and public emotional investment in the issues is widespread. Media coverage is often sensational because it finds resonance in readers' fears and experiences – so that we think crime is more widespread than it is and underestimate the severity of the courts' response. The government has taken the lead, expressly arguing for a 'rebalancing of the criminal justice system'. Speaking in 2002, the Prime Minister Tony Blair identified six 'key components' of the government's strategy:

- tackling causes,
- cracking down on anti-social behaviour,
- drugs,
- organised crime,
- reform of the criminal justice system,
- police reducing crime.[8]

Undoubtedly, this covers a number of the key issues facing the system. However, in addition, the government correctly identified a 'justice gap'.[9] Its own statistics revealed that as little as 20 per cent of recorded crimes led to an arrest, with recorded crime accounting for less than ten per cent of the total number of crimes committed.

Garland suggests that issues surrounding victims and public safety have come to dominate policy because people feel they have a right to be protected from crime when traditional safety nets – such as job security, pensions, the welfare state and family structures – have largely disappeared. Equally, crime statistics are seen as being unreliable, often misleading and unable to provide reassurance. The forthcoming Victims and Witnesses Bill acknowledges the growing political importance of victims, by aiming to ensure that information and consultation is available consistently across England and Wales, and that respect for victims is enhanced. Arguably, this will not add to arrangements that should be in place anyway. In the light of these factors, public dissatisfaction is readily understandable.

There is a general consensus that crime must be tackled seriously. However, the concern is that we have been trying to do this by relying on increasingly heavier penalties, when there is little empirical evidence that these have worked. The result is that prisons become more ineffective, under the weight of supporting far greater numbers than were ever intended, frustrating what rehabilitative potential they have. Policy-making becomes increasingly punitive. There is no realistic way to reverse this unless credible alternatives to custody are available and acceptable. Nor is prison itself an isolated phenomenon – it is unlikely to achieve results without follow-on work in the community. The value of resettlement has become clearer but there remains a lack of both social structures and cultural values that desperately needs to be acknowledged by society as a whole. Awakening cultural sensibilities and addressing this lack of social structures is a challenge for restorative practice, when the long-term needs of victims, offenders, and society are disregarded in favour of short-term, illusory, reassurance.

Prisons and statistics

In 1993, the prison population in England and Wales was 44,566. In June 2003 it was 73,379 – its highest ever recorded level. The UK now has the highest imprisonment rate in the EU at 139 per 100,000; we have overtaken Portugal (131) and now imprison a significantly higher proportion of our population than our near neighbours Ireland and France (86 and 85 per 100,000 respectively).[10] Worse still, the Home Office estimates that, even on favourable assumptions, numbers will reach 91,400 by 2009.[11]

The Prison Reform Trust believes this rise is caused by significant increases in the number of offenders sent to prison and in the length of sentences. For example, in 1993, one defendant in 26 would have received a custodial sentence, now this figure is one in 13. Between 1991 and 2002, the number of adult prisoners sentenced to 12 months or less more than doubled to over 49,000. The number of long-term prisoners has increased considerably. In 1992, 3,000 prisoners were serving life sentences, now there are 5,352. We have the highest number of life-sentence prisoners in Western Europe. However, the increased use of custodial sentences has not reduced re-offending rates. Fifty-nine per cent of prisoners are reconvicted within two years of release. The reconviction rate for male young adults (those under 21) is 74 per cent and for prisoners sentenced for burglary is 75 per cent.

Research commissioned by the Home Office[12] tells us that people can sometimes be deterred from crime, but the evidence is that likelihood of conviction is a much greater deterrent than length of sentence. Punishment *certainty*, rather than *severity*, is what influences crime trends. In conclusion, the current emphasis on longer sentences has little relevance or effect, given the apparent difficulty of greatly increasing the probability of conviction rates – ie, reducing the 'justice gap'. It is an expensive way to worsen the situation, and can do nothing to assist victims or, indeed, public protection in the longer term.

Social exclusion

A snapshot view of the prison population[13] shows us the role that social exclusion plays in offending behaviour. Literacy and numeracy levels are significantly lower than in the general population as a whole: 65 per cent of prisoners have a numeracy level at or below that expected of an 11-year-old (compared to 23 per cent of the general population) and 48 per cent have a reading level at or below that expected of an 11-year-old (compared to 21 per cent in the general population). Other statistics are similarly striking: 52 per cent of male prisoners and 71 per cent of female prisoners have no qualifications (compared to 15 per cent generally); 32 per cent are homeless (0.9 per cent); 27 per cent had been taken into care as children (2 per cent); 67 per cent were unemployed before imprisonment (5 per cent); and 72 per cent of male prisoners and 70 per cent of female prisoners are suffering from two or more mental disorders (5 per cent and 2 per cent respectively).

There is no mention in the report[14] of restorative justice, only that 'action in and after prison should be the single best way to tackle the persistent offenders who commit the bulk of recorded crime'. Restorative interventions before sentence, as we shall see, could be invaluable.

Women in prison

The number of women in prison has risen by 191 per cent in the last ten years: from 1,577 in 1993 to 4,554 in June 2003; 21 per cent are on remand and one in five is acquitted. In 1992, 38 per cent were reconvicted within two years, now this figure is 53 per cent. Only 15 per cent of women prisoners are held for violent offences.

Concern about these figures has prompted wider research and the Prison Reform Trust's Wedderburn inquiry and *Troubled Inside* reports[15] are the source of some telling statistics. Up to 50 per cent of women in prison had experienced domestic violence (twice the rate of the general population); 54 per cent on remand and 41 per cent sentenced had been drug-dependent in the year before they went to prison; 38 per cent had used alcohol excessively; 50 per cent of women clinically interviewed were thought to have personality disorders; and 31 per cent were thought to have antisocial personality disorders. At least one-third had suffered sexual abuse; 21 per cent had been living alone with dependent children; and 66 per cent had dependent children. The propensity of women in custody to harm themselves is well-documented and suicide rates in prison are currently at their highest level.

These figures show the extent of the problems we are facing, and are testament to the failure of current policy. Serious penalties cannot compensate for not taking causes seriously; and prisons are so overcrowded that any rehabilitative potential they may have is severely limited. Moreover, there is now a consensus that short prison sentences are disruptive and have overwhelmingly negative effects.

The Criminal Justice Act 2003

The Criminal Justice Act 2003 aims to reduce the number and length of short sentences by introducing new measures:

- custody plus (where sentences of under 12 months will be replaced by a short period in custody, of up to three months, followed by a longer period of supervision in the community);
- the increased use of deferred sentences, to explore the scope for restorative justice; and
- intermittent sentences, where offenders will serve their sentences in short blocks of a few days at a time.

We have already seen an extension of electronic tagging and, with more sophisticated methods of surveillance available all the time, it is surprising that there is still support (and willingness to pay for) more prison building, especially when it does not reduce crime or the fear of crime.

Court of Appeal guidelines

The Lord Chief Justice, Lord Woolf, issued Court of Appeal guidelines for sentencing burglars last year and urged the use of community-based sentences rather than a few months' imprisonment. He argued that community penalties could be more beneficial and at the same time help to halt the growth of the prison population. New guidance urges magistrates to consider community penalties rather than custodial sentences for driving while disqualified, burglary and theft.

These are welcome initiatives but nobody would pretend that they are enough. The Criminal Justice Act 2003 contains further measures that will lengthen sentences and supervision; life sentences are also lengthening. The picture is bleak and this report will argue that, in a situation that is clearly deteriorating, restorative justice presents us with an opportunity to reverse these trends, which are as destructive for society and victims as they are for offenders. The following chapter examines what restorative justice is, and how it works.

Notes

1 *A Review of the Criminal Courts of England and Wales* (TSO, October 2001).

2 Ibid, at para 69.

3 *Restorative Justice: the government's strategy* (TSO, July 2003).

4 Ibid, executive summary.

5 Ibid, para 1.1.

6 See Kathleen Daly, 'Conferencing in Australia and New Zealand: variations, research findings and prospects', *Restorative Justice for Juveniles: conferencing, mediation and Circles* (Edited by Maxwell and Morris, Hart Publishing, 2001).

7 Eg, David Garland, 'The Culture of Higher Crime Societies', *British Journal of Criminology*.

8 Speech, 18 June 2002.

9 'Criminal Justice System', *Narrowing the Justice Gap* (2001).

10 Prison Reform Trust *Briefing*, June 2003 (quoting Home Office statistics).

11 Prison Reform Trust *Annual Report 2002*.

12 Von Hirsch, Bottoms, Burney and Wilkstrom (University of Cambridge, Institute of Criminology, Hart Publishing, 1999).

13 See the Social Exclusion Unit's Report, *Reducing Reoffending by Ex-Prisoners*, July 2002.

14 Ibid.

15. F Farrant, *Troubled inside: Responding to the needs of children and young people in prison*, Prison Reform Trust (2002), D Rickford, *Troubled inside: Responding to the mental health needs of women in prison*, Prison Reform Trust (2003), *Justice for women: the need for reform*, Prison Reform Trust (2000)

Chapter 2 – Definitions, models and principles

In the previous chapter, we considered the government's definition of restorative justice. Tony Marshall, an early pioneer, provides a more discursive version in his overview of restorative justice, published by the Home Office in 1999:[1]

> [It] is a problem-solving approach to crime which involves the parties themselves, and the community generally, in an active relationship with statutory agencies.

He further described it as:

> A process whereby all parties with a stake in a particular offence come together to resolve collectively how to deal with the aftermath of an offence and its implications for the future.

The view from Australia, where restorative justice is more established, is that it is hard to define. Commentators[2] say that:

> It emphasises the repair of harms and of ruptured social bonds resulting from crime; it focuses on the relationships between crime, victims, offenders and society; its practices will necessitate changes in how state officials work, both what they do and how they do it.

These definitions and descriptions are not immediately clear, as the meaning will need to be worked out in the context of individual circumstances and methods. However, restorative practice aims to address the particular (and reasonable) needs and wishes of those participating. It is best understood in terms of the values it espouses and, logically, our understanding is likely to improve with exposure to these values and with experience of their implementation.

Marshall and Daly point out the essentials for restorative justice: that it is inclusive of victims and presents a new focus on victim-offender dialogue. This is seen as a way to resolve offences and their consequences more constructively, with reference to the wider community, and with the aid of direct participation by those involved. Restorative justice aims to replace the notion that criminal justice is a matter between state and offender, with the idea that victim, community and offender should own the process. Marshall lists the five primary objectives of this approach:

- attending to the needs of victims;
- preventing reoffending by reintegrating the offender into the community;
- enabling offenders to assume responsibility for their actions;
- recreating communities that can support victims, rehabilitate offenders and actively prevent further crime; and
- avoiding the escalation of the mechanisms of justice and the associated costs and delays.

In theory, these objectives represent a move away from the punitive ethos, towards a more holistic approach that seeks to match the making of amends with offenders' and victims' circumstances. It is important to stress that this may well have a punitive element but, because the parties will have a chance to speak directly for themselves, the facts, their background, and the human experiences surrounding offences will be better known. Offenders are more likely to comply with negotiated agreements in which they have played a part, and during which they have heard victims' views and feelings, than with sanctions imposed by courts. In the process of negotiation and exchange, offenders are thought to find it easier to take responsibility than if they were appearing at court.

Maxwell and Morris,[3] both well-known experts in New Zealand, have articulated a further five key principles at the core of restorative practice. These are:

- full participation and consensus of all parties;
- aiming to heal what is broken (trust and relationships);
- full and direct accountability (meaning explanations of the full facts and background);
- aiming to reunite what has been divided (restoring damage to the community); and
- strengthening communities to prevent further harm.

This is new and unfamiliar language in a sphere that has long been dominated by an adversarial legal perspective but it aims to describe the possibilities of a problem-solving approach, seeking to put a human face on crucial transactions between individuals and society. These are the central values, which may be more easily illustrated (below) by considering some of the methods used to implement them.

Models of restorative practice

There are many types of restorative intervention and, as we shall see, they may be introduced at a number of different stages in the criminal justice process. However, the principal models are:

- victim empathy programmes,
- victim-offender mediation,
- restorative conferencing and cautioning,
- family group conferencing,
- sentencing circles (also known as peacemaking or community circles).

Victim empathy programmes

These programmes prepare offenders to participate in restorative processes with or without victims. They guide offenders towards considering their own behaviour from the perspective of their victims. Participants may be asked to reflect on their own feelings of victimisation at earlier times in their lives (many offenders will themselves have been assaulted, abused, or offended against). They are then encouraged to think about all those affected by their behaviour, such as families, friends and the wider community as well as their immediate victims.

Programmes may be run in partnership with organisations such as Victim Support and approaches may be varied, possibly including Victim Impact Panels. These are fora for offenders and victim representatives to communicate directly with each other, in order to familiarise themselves with their own and others' feelings and experiences.

Victim-offender mediation

Victim-offender mediation derives its effectiveness from dialogue between the parties. It may be direct (where the parties meet) or indirect (where they do not), facilitated by a mediator, in order to try to resolve the issues and questions raised by the offence. Preparation is essential to make sure that both parties are clear about the process and ground rules, are aware of what may happen, and of the objectives of the meeting. The ground rules require respectful language and behaviour; a consensus to work towards resolution rather than conflict; an emphasis on putting things right, and reaching realistic and proportionate agreements; and are necessary to ensure that the mediator retains control. Offenders can thus explain the context of offences and victims can detail the consequences in their own time, before the meeting moves on to more direct exchanges, within a framework of restoration and accountability. Mediation usually involves the parties being alone together, although some family members or supporters may attend. This is where victim-offender mediation differs from conferencing (discussed below), where many more people may be invited to meetings. Indirect mediation may be appropriate where, for example, victims do not want to meet offenders but do want to convey the impact that the offence has had on them via the mediator. Equally, it may be the better option where an offender is lacking in remorse, or so damaged (and therefore lacking in empathy) that a meeting is unlikely to be constructive. See further chapter 6, where victim-offender mediation is already a fairly established feature of both the Austrian and Norwegian systems.

Restorative conferencing

Restorative conferences are meetings for victims, offenders and their supporters, including family, friends, teachers or youth workers. They have a different structure from mediation and within the UK have mainly been used by Thames Valley Police. Police facilitators usually use scripted questions designed to help the parties give their accounts of the offence, its background and its effects. The conclusion will be a caution but the process tries to promote understanding of the human context and consequences of events. Restorative conferencing is considered further in chapter 9 and we note that the Justice Research Consortium is running a pilot scheme for more serious offences.

Restorative cautioning

Restorative cautioning follows the same pattern as conferencing: however, victims are not present.

Family group conferencing

Family group conferencing similarly involves meetings of offenders and victims, together with their family and supporters. They are convened by completely independent facilitators and have so far been used mostly with young people. This represents another means of examining the same subject matter and issues. The idea is the same: to reach agreements that will include reparation, and attempt to promote the development of the young person in order to minimise the risk of reoffending.

Conferences begin with the parties giving their account of events and feelings, and any relevant background. Any professionals present will make their contributions and then families and supporters can have their say. Plans are then constructed to address the needs for reparation and reintegration. These may be agreed in a number of ways, according to the jurisdiction in which they are operating, and must generally be ratified by courts, youth offender panels, or similar bodies. See chapters 4, 5 and 8 for a review of conference practice in New Zealand and Australia, the USA, and England and Wales, respectively.

Sentencing circles

Sentencing circles are strictly part of the court process. They deal with suitable cases referred to them after conviction. They are community-based interventions that seek to develop appropriate sentencing plans, using traditional circle ritual and structure.[4] Everyone has the opportunity to speak without interruption but, in addition to offenders, victims, and their supporters, judges and support staff are also necessary.

Heino Lilles, writing about sentencing circles in Canada,[5] stresses that they should be restricted to motivated offenders who have the support of the community, and for serious offences that justify significant interventions, because they are time-consuming and costly to operate. Unlike many other restorative justice processes, convictions are recorded and past history is taken into account. It is worth listing their principal characteristics. Although there are many procedural variations, they differ in important respects from other models under discussion. The key points are that:

- any criminal record or other reports should be exhibited;
- a record should be made of proceedings;
- disputed facts should be judicially determined by taking evidence under oath;
- they should be open to the public;
- participation should be voluntary;
- the offender can be legally represented, and can address the circle;
- the media can attend and report proceedings;
- circle participants must have copies of pre-sentence reports, etc;
- judges should impose sentence, in accordance with the law; and
- sentences are subject to appeal in the usual way.

General principles

All these methods have principles in common, in keeping with their restorative intentions. Confidentiality applies to all proceedings. If communication breaks down, or agreements are not made or fulfilled, cases will usually be returned to the formal system. In this event, everything starts from the beginning again, and nothing that has been said is admissible in court.

Judicial oversight is another central factor. It varies as to how much this is built into interventions in the systems being considered. However, courts generally play a background role, deciding upon facts which may be disputed, or acting as supervisory bodies where agreements cannot be reached or are dishonoured. They have been described as a 'safety net': checking that outcomes are broadly acceptable and that the quality of decision-making is sufficiently high. Judges need to be aware of the philosophy of restorative justice and check whether agreements are the result of negotiation and participation and whether, for example, a sufficient number of supporters have attended to ensure this. They may also want to be satisfied that legal advice has been sought at some point before the restorative process. However, they should be reluctant to intervene unless agreements are too extreme in either direction.

In theory, engagement with restorative processes should be voluntary. However, if they are now to be incorporated into a coercive criminal justice system, it is doubtful how voluntary participation can really be. Many defendants may seek to avoid the trauma and uncertainty of court hearings by admitting offences that they could successfully defend. Practitioners acknowledge that volunteering is unrealistic in this context and now talk in terms of 'informed consent' for offenders, and ' informed choice' for victims, rather than voluntary agreement. International practice seems to be developing on this basis.

The role of lawyers is generally restricted to advising before and after restorative interventions, except in sentencing circles, which are discussed further in chapter 3. In some countries they may be present part of the time but they will usually facilitate and advise rather than represent or test the evidence. The momentum for restorative practice stems from work with young people, and many youth justice systems are now clearly organised around the best interests of the child, which lawyers must also work towards.

Community participation is another important theme and, again, this can mean different things in different places. Sometimes, community representatives are carefully chosen. At others, arrangements seem much more haphazard, with considerable potential for affecting outcomes. The part played by volunteers in some systems represents community involvement and there are different attitudes as to whether mediators/facilitators should be paid employees (who may professionalise restorative responses) or whether the use of volunteers is indispensable to maintaining community involvement.

Benefits and shortcomings

These methods of working at the interface between victim and offender are the centrepiece of restorative practice. They aim to provide space for free-flowing discussions before trial or sentence, allowing people the opportunity to describe their feelings about offences and their consequences, and to have a voice in shaping outcomes. However, as our collective experience of victim-offender dialogue grows, its advantages and disadvantages become clearer. We attempt to summarise these below, before considering international and domestic practice in more detail.

Potential strengths

The keynote of restorative justice is informality. This allows for a creative, flexible, problem-solving approach. Meetings – where the parties come face-to-face with each other as human beings – can break down preconceived ideas and stereotypes. They encourage victims to articulate the harm they have suffered and for offenders to provide a context for their actions. A full knowledge of the perspectives of all parties can promote greater understanding, allowing the victim to move on and the offender to reintegrate. It can access such positive qualities as empathy, reconciliation, forgiveness, and genuine apology. Examples where these were achieved – after years of disenchantment with formal court proceedings – prompted the euphoria that originally helped to spread and publicise restorative justice. Results can be durable and, where agreements are kept, there may be a positive impact on reoffending.

Potential weaknesses

However, other examples have now shown that a space for creativity may also prove to be a forum for more destructive purposes. Anger, resentment and hostility will not automatically wither away in the face of good intentions. Meetings may also release negative emotions resulting in humiliation, domination by one party, stigma, demoralisation and revictimisation.

Heather Strang, in her recent survey from the point of view of victims,[6] finds that, in general, restorative practice is only likely to be beneficial 'if conditions are right on both sides'. Nevertheless, victims may be more afraid as a result of a conference, for example, of retaliation. They may experience an imbalance of power at the meeting and may feel 'used' in order to reform the offender. There may also be a limit on the reparation or restoration that is possible. For example, offenders cannot restore teeth that they may have broken in an assault. The more serious the offence, the more obvious the limits become.

Lessons learned

Strang lists the lessons learned from failed conferences. The evidence suggests that steps should be taken to avoid:

- poor police work (for example, overestimating the acceptance of responsibility by the offender);
- insufficient preparation of victims and offenders;
- poor conference organisation (victims may be intimidated by sharing the same room with the offender prior to the meeting);
- inadequate training of facilitators (for example, personal prejudices, inappropriate interventions, or ignoring relevant history);
- lack of follow-up of conference agreements (it is important to notify victims when they have been honoured); and
- an excessive focus on the offender, resulting in insufficient attention for the victim.

Strang's research is generally encouraging. She finds that victims usually feel safer after conferences, with their fear and anger falling as their sympathy and security rises. They have stronger feelings of dignity, self-confidence and self-respect. They receive more apologies and their desire for revenge is allayed. Strang's optimism is shared by those we met running projects and systems in the course of our research. However, now that restorative justice is becoming mainstream, we recognise the need to be clear about its potential failings, as well as reporting on the undoubted enthusiasm in the field, before important decisions about implementation are made.

Specialist areas

Female offenders

The government's strategy document highlights the different considerations, which may affect implementation in relation to domestic violence, race hate and homophobia cases. Attitudes are divided, but there is some evidence that restorative methods may be particularly beneficial with female offenders if they help to deal with issues of abuse and relationships. These often underlie offending and are further discussed in chapters 5 and 6. However, there are potential difficulties, in that women seem more likely to accept an excess of responsibility, leading to overwhelming feelings of guilt and possible self harm. These are areas where specific work and further research would be useful.

Domestic violence

Domestic violence is a problem of enormous social proportion. The number of unrecorded cases is high and, where allegations are prosecuted, complainants often withdraw for a variety of understandable reasons. It is common ground that new approaches are needed and in recent years police attitudes have changed to reflect this. There are a number of experiments underway with differently constituted domestic violence courts.

It is now more widely recognised that the effects of violence in the home may be disastrous for children and encourage them to offend similarly and otherwise. They may suffer repeat victimisation and their development is likely to be prejudiced by witnessing such detrimental methods of resolving conflicts.[7] The trauma and damage experienced by many women is now better documented, but no less serious.

This is a setting where one party will almost certainly be weaker than the other, and where recidivism is normal. This has influenced international views on the appropriateness of mediation, although it has also now been identified as a challenge. Bannenberg and Rossner indicate the ideas that need to be tried:[8]

- regulating conflicts by victim-offender mediation;
- aiming to strengthen the weaker party; or
- confronting the offender without the victim having to be present.

What is needed, they argue, is to improve victims' protection, to prevent conflicts from escalating, and to prevent future violence. This is best attempted with an eye to the criminal law if it should not succeed via mediation.

A high percentage of violent crime and homicides are attributable to domestic violence. A variety of responses, including anti-aggression training and other specialised initiatives, are indispensable if headway is to be made to reduce violence among people who may well have suffered from it themselves. It is particularly important, therefore, to be aware of the special problems that may manifest themselves in mediation. These include:

- victims being exposed to offenders in face-to-face meetings;
- victims finding it difficult to express and enforce their rights;
- mediators' neutrality being compromised by attempts to balance the power between the parties; and
- difficulties in meeting the needs or demands for surveillance.

Domestic violence cases are often the product of a long history of violence and this makes them more intractable. Where mediation is attempted, as in Austria see chapter 6, it is likely that two mediators will be considered necessary and it will take more time, more preparation, and more sessions. Accumulated wisdom[9] supports taking a stand against violence and drawing attention to the weaker position of the victim during negotiations. Methods may have to be devised to even-out the imbalance of power, for example, by limiting talking time, assisting the articulation of interests, and having recourse to pre-formulated comments. Links must also be made with other institutions offering aid and advice, and mediators should reach agreements with victims to report any renewed violence within a specified time period.

It follows that greater specialisation in victim-offender services is needed. It is suggested[10] that in order to encourage men (who may be reluctant) to participate, it may be necessary to point to the alternative of prosecution – a course which should certainly be taken if there is repeat violence. These are general concerns, which call for discussion, but they are highlighted in this context and probably in the race hate and homophobia contexts also.

Austria is one of the few countries where domestic violence cases are routinely mediated and, even then, they are carefully screened. Their system is described in chapter 6. We conclude that this is an area – like the others referred to in the government's strategy paper – where specialised methods and training should be employed, at least by way of experimentation.

Notes

1 Marshall, *Restorative Justice: an overview* (Home Office, 1999).
2 Daly and Immarigeon, 1998.
3 Maxwell and Morris, *Restorative Justice for Juveniles* (Hart Publishing, 2001).
4 Members sit in a circle and pass round a talking piece (eg, a stone or feather). Only the person holding the talking piece may speak. For more information see B Stuart, 'Guiding Principles for Peacemaking Circles', *Restorative Community Justice* (G Bazemore and M Schiff (eds), Anderson, 2001).

5 See Maxwell and Morris, 'Circle Sentencing: part of the restorative justice continuum',
Restorative Justice for Juveniles (Hart Publishing, 2001).
6 *Repair or Revenge* (Clarendon, 2002).
7 see Bannenberg and Rossner, 'New Developments in Restorative Justice to handle Family
Violence', *Restorative Justice in Context: international practice and directions* (Weitekamp and
Kerner (eds), Willan Publishing, 2003).
8 Ibid.
9 Ibid.
10 Ibid.

Chapter 3 – Human rights and accountability

Although human rights have not been at the forefront of discussions about the development of restorative practice, nevertheless, they provide the principles and legal framework within which it must operate. Attention to safeguards is especially important in informal structures as these are necessary to prevent any abuse, which may arise from poor standards or misperception of aims. Legal challenges have so far been few but international human rights law, in the form of conventions drafted since the 1960s, has had a hugely proactive effect. These conventions have created and sustained a momentum towards restorative practice, arising out of their consideration of youth justice and children's rights generally. This is the area in which restorative justice began and the discussion that follows is therefore based on that experience. However, there is now an accelerating interest in the application of restorative methods to adults and, again, this is an international trend which is likely to continue.

After some scepticism, there is now growing support among the judiciary and the legal profession for restorative approaches. The Lord Chief Justice, Lord Woolf, attended a sentencing circle at a flagship conference in Winchester in 2001. Since then, he has presided over a Court of Appeal that agreed to reduce a sentence by two years because of the productivity of the victim-offender dialogue that had taken place.[1] The meeting was attended by the family members of both parties. The court observed that it was 'by no means a soft option' and went on to conclude that restorative justice 'which was designed to ensure effective sentencing for the better protection of the public, appeared to be going at least some way to achieving its purpose and should be encouraged'.

Familiarity with these ideas is growing and practice is being extended rapidly. This chapter considers some of the human rights factors that have to be taken into account in what is now a continuing process.

Human rights

The Human Rights Act 1998 brought into effect many of the principles of the European Convention on Human Rights and the earlier Universal Declaration of Human Rights on which it was based. These principles were devised as a direct result of the gross human rights violations of the Second World War. Its provisions stressed, understandably, the importance of due process and of protection from arbitrariness, disproportionality and discrimination. Young people were not the uppermost concern of the drafters and the lack of provisions relating to them has been remedied by other, more specific, international conventions. The rights of victims and witnesses were equally unconsidered, although subsequent jurisprudence, and indeed practice (the family of James Bulger was allowed to make submissions to the European Court), has gone some way to filling the gap.

Some provisions of the European Convention on Human Rights are directly relevant to restorative justice, because they relate to criminal proceedings, sentencing, and respect for privacy – establishing standards to which criminal (including restorative) justice must have regard. They are:

- article 6 – requiring a fair trial and due process of law;
- article 5 – guaranteeing the right to liberty (which can only be interfered with for specified and legally-based purposes); and
- article 8 – providing for the right to respect for a private and family life (important in relation to both victims and offenders in restorative practice).

These provisions, and those of relevant international conventions, are set out in Appendix 1. Case-law confirms that these rights apply to children as well as adults.[2]

Article 6 primarily applies where proceedings are contested. However, it is worth summarising the principles that have developed, even though restorative practice only becomes relevant after admissions of responsibility or guilt. So far, legal assistance and representation – a pre-requisite of fair trial (or sentence) – has attracted the most attention.[3] Below, we review some of the points made by recent case-law and consider their implications.

Case-law
The Venables and Thompson case
The decision of the European Court[4] in the case of Venables and Thompson is the best publicised and most important recent legal development in relation to trials (and by implication sentencing) of children and young people. It establishes crucial principles, which have a key influence on policy and practice. The case involved two ten-year-old boys who were convicted, by an adult Crown Court, of murdering the toddler James Bulger. They were sentenced to detention at Her Majesty's pleasure, and the then Home Secretary Michael Howard set

their tariffs (minimum term of detention) at a significantly higher figure than that envisaged by the trial judge and Lord Chief Justice.

The questions for the court were whether the Home Secretary's role was compatible with the obligation under article 6 to provide an independent and impartial tribunal, and whether the boys' trial in an adult court had been fair. It found that the Home Secretary, as a member of the executive, should have no part to play in the sentencing process. Furthermore, it ruled that the trial had not been fair and it identified 'effective participation' as an essential requirement of article 6. The court said that to make such participation possible:

> it is essential that a child charged with an offence is dealt with in a manner which takes full account of his age, level of maturity and intellectual and emotional capacities.

Account should be taken of potential limitations such as the inability to instruct lawyers, to testify adequately in one's own defence, and to take decisions in one's own best interests. These will be relevant in restorative processes, such as youth offender panels (see chapter 8), which should already be taking the capacity of the participants into account.

The Lanark case

Children's hearings in Scotland have been operating without legal representation since 1971. These involve young people who have offended or who may be in need of child protection. They appear before a panel of three lay people. The idea was that flexible, creative, child-centred solutions would be easier to reach in direct dialogue with the child and this thinking has been applied to youth offender panels. This has now been challenged following the implementation of the Human Rights Act 1998. The decision by the Scottish Court of Session[5] (in what was referred to as 'the Lanark case') suggests that lack of legal representation at children's hearings could, in certain cases, amount to a breach of article 6 and that panels may have discretion to grant such representation.

What is at issue is the capacity of the child to understand and participate meaningfully in the proceedings, as identified by the *Venables and Thompson* ruling. Serious emotional, psychological or intellectual problems – all are especially prevalent in young people appearing before courts – may prove a significant disadvantage in these respects, thus triggering the protection of article 6 and requiring legal representation. This decision could be invoked to support a challenge about the lack of such representation at young offenders' panels.

The R (on the application of U) v MPC case[6]

The U case concerned an application by a young person who had been reprimanded and his name placed on the sex offenders' register. Reprimands and final warnings were introduced by the Crime and Disorder Act 1998 (see chapter 8) as the first and second responses to minor offending by young people who accepted their justification. U became the subject of these new arrangements, apparently not realising their consequences. He applied to the High Court, which ruled that a young person who accepts a reprimand must be fully advised of the consequences. If, in the circumstances of the offence, the offender is to be placed on the statutory sex offenders' register he must be specifically informed if the reprimand is to be lawful. Otherwise, the court decided, it would breach article 6.

This decision again demonstrates the importance that courts will give to defendants being fully informed and able to comprehend, so that consent is effective and decisions can properly be reached. It is another pointer to access to legal representation in such circumstances.

International conventions

More recent international conventions than the UN Declaration and the European Convention have specifically recognised the special needs of young people, as well as their rights. The International Covenant on Civil and Political Rights, ratified by the UK in 1976, provided that young people charged with offences should be separated from adults, their age should be taken account of, and their rehabilitation promoted.[7]

The UN Standard Minimum Rules for the Administration of Juvenile Justice (commonly known as the 'Beijing Rules') date from 1985. They expound a regime that combines requirements for due process of law[8] with consideration of the interests and future development of the child.[9] Significantly, they recognise the 'special needs of juveniles' and therefore the need for a flexible range of options in dealing with and sentencing young offenders.[10] They underline the importance of diversion and flexibility, as well as the undesirability of formal trial[11] and detention. Privacy and anonymity are declared necessary to prevent the harmful and counter-productive effects of stigma and labelling[12] and records are required to be kept confidential, and not used in adult proceedings.[13] The rules insist on continuing research and evaluation in order to monitor and refine systems and to ensure effectiveness and flexibility.[14]

These standards have influenced policy, practice and legislation around the world, and the Austrian Juvenile Justice Act of 1989 (see chapter 6) is based on them. The Committee of Ministers of the Council of Europe issued a Recommendation[15] on social reactions to juvenile delinquency in response, indicating that education and social integration should be an indispensable part of penal systems for juveniles, and urging Member States to review their legislation and practice with this in mind.

Even better known than the Beijing Rules is the International Convention on the Rights of the Child (ICRC), which was introduced in 1989 and came into force in 1990. This deals with a wide range of children's rights and has been ratified almost universally.

The ICRC begins from the point that the rights of the child are paramount, so that any curtailment of rights or freedoms must have as its aim the best interests of the child. Children should participate in decision-making that affects them. This is a principle adopted by reformers in New Zealand (see chapter 4) and has been extremely influential internationally. It challenges the assumption that due process alone can protect vulnerable and developing young people and asserts their need to be treated differently, and for their reintegration into society to be promoted. Article 40 declares the aims of an appropriate youth justice system:

> States Parties recognise the rights of every child alleged as, accused of, or recognised as having infringed the penal law to be treated in a manner consistent with the promotion of the child's sense of dignity and worth, which reinforces the child's respect for the human rights and fundamental freedoms of others and which takes into account the child's age and the desirability of promoting the child's reintegration and the child's assuming a constructive role in society.[16]

The convention acknowledges the need for procedural safeguards – including legal advice – for younger accused persons in criminal cases,[17] and recommends that they be dealt with out of court 'providing that human rights and safeguards are fully respected'.[18] It advocates the need for alternatives to institutions, 'to ensure that children are dealt with in a manner appropriate both to their circumstances and the offence',[19] for a sparing and minimum use of detention,[20] and that they should be able to participate and be heard in any proceedings relating to them.[21]

In 1990, the UN Guidelines for the Protection of Juvenile Delinquency (known as 'the Riyadh Guidelines') and the UN Rules for the Protection of Juveniles Deprived of their Liberty confirmed that criminalisation should be avoided for behaviour not causing serious damage to the development of the child or harm to others.[22] They insisted that:

> Youth justice systems should uphold the rights and safety and promote the
> physical and mental well-being of juveniles.[23]

These are some of the ideas that have underpinned and sustained the movement towards restorative justice for young people. The part they have played in its genesis has been fundamental. This is significant, from the point of view that, following the Human Rights Act, both the domestic courts and Strasbourg are more receptive to international human rights instruments. For example, both the House of Lords and the European Court of Human Rights endorsed principles from the ICRC in their separate considerations of the *Venables and Thompson* case (see above), suggesting that this trend is on the increase.

There are many issues still to be tested but it is useful to bear in mind, while considering human rights standards, the roles of courts, victims and communities in restorative practice. The status of processes (whether they are criminal processes resulting in a criminal record or voluntary agreements that provide reparation and resolution) and their outcomes are equally important. It is these factors, as well as the provision of legal advice and representation, which may potentially have an unbalancing effect triggering human rights violations.

Accountability

Within a human rights framework, accountability is of central importance for developing practice. As we have seen, transformation and success are not assured: restorative interventions do not operate in a vacuum. Training, resources for courses, drug treatment programmes and other necessary follow-on measures are fundamental to the achievement of objectives. Standards of practice, built firmly on restorative values, are clearly indispensable. Roche,[24] an Australian academic and commentator, argues that we must be careful not to create systems based on utopian visions with no reference to objective standards and, therefore, that accountability is vital to bridge the gap between optimism and reality.

Roche's view is that the acceptability of meetings should depend on the quality of the decision-making process, itself dependent on effective participation by all parties. Outcomes must be reasoned and reasonable and they must comply with upper and lower limits – a refinement (that has gained explicit acceptance) of the original idea that outcomes should reflect the participants' needs and wishes alone. These are key human rights concepts and it is argued[25] that the novelty of restorative practice is that it is a deliberative democratic process to reach and enforce sentencing agreements that have the potential to be more productive.

In order to achieve this, the accounts given by participants at meetings have to be rigorously and sensitively scrutinised and assessed by everybody present and there must be credible judicial oversight. This is crucial to the quality and legitimacy of decision-making. In addition, accountability must be persuasive rather than directive, and must avoid domination – moving forward by means of deliberation, justification and exchange. Facilitators will need good judgment about when and whether to intervene and must use the essential requirement for effective participation as their guide. There will be difficulties. The threat of prosecution remains if the meeting goes wrong and, in itself, it is a communicative process that clearly favours the articulate and confident. It can easily be humiliating for young offenders and risk re-victimising victims. Conferences will only be acceptable, to repeat Heather Strang's[26] view, 'if conditions are right on both sides'.

Guidelines and standards

Guidelines and standards are obviously necessary but, while recognising this, commentators have also expressed reservations about making them too prescriptive. The challenge is that flexibility also needs to be preserved in order to deal with each case in the most sensitive way. There is a tension here between the need for clear parameters for the protection of the parties and a more creative, individualised approach. Roche[27] suggests that deliberative accountability can be enhanced by:

- consensual decision-making;
- a diverse range of participants (to improve scrutiny and reality-test);
- the presence of observers;
- meetings that are neither too big nor too long;
- the representation of community interests; and
- the encouragement of expression in relaxed and unthreatening terms.

He adds voluntariness to this list, inasmuch as it can be achieved, and recognises that preparation, legal advice and the presence of supporters are all important ingredients to the quality of the process.

In 1999, the International Scientific and Professional Advisory Council of the United Nations released a paper entitled *An Overview of Restorative Justice Programmes and Issues*, drafted by Professor Paul Friday. The study concluded:

> *Guidelines and Standards are desperately needed. There is a danger that programs that are initially restorative in outlook recreate the courtroom process and, in turn, undermine rather than cultivate restoration. There is also the danger that the legal basis for initiating the process can get lost. And there is a third danger that the etiological factors producing crime – poverty, racism, cultural/social values, individualism will not be addressed as they are uncovered in the process.[28]*

A Council of Europe Recommendation Concerning Mediation in Penal Matters was adopted in 1999[29] and in 2001 the European Communities' framework decision on restorative justice[30] was published. Article 10 requires member states to promote mediation in criminal cases for appropriate offences; to ensure that any agreement between victim and offender reached in the course of such mediation is taken into account; and (under article 17) to put into place laws, regulations and administrative provisions to comply with the framework decision by March 2006. Almost simultaneously the Victim-Offender Mediation Association published *Recommended Ethical Guidelines*.[31] The United Nations Economic and Social Council (ESOC) subsequently endorsed *Basic Principles for Restorative Justice*[32] in July 2002, adding that all Member States should consider establishing guidelines governing restorative programmes. The Expert Group of the UN ESOC agreed that the purpose of basic principles was to assist Member States of the UN to adopt and standardise restorative justice initiatives in their justice systems but that these should not be mandatory or prescriptive.

Within the UK, the Restorative Justice Consortium produced a *Statement of Restorative Justice Principles* in March 2002.[33] A broad set of standards for safe and effective restorative practice is emerging and the various reports really only differ in detail. The government's new national strategy shows that it accepts these arguments and that by funding more research and initiating pilot schemes we will learn to connect theory and practice, and to establish a continuing dialogue of good practice. This challenge must be met if we are to deliver high-quality, effective practice with long-term benefit.

Practice

We turn now to how these principles and standards are implemented in a range of different settings, countries and cultures.

Notes

1 *R v Collins* (2003) *Times* 14 April.
2 See, eg, *Nielsen v Denmark* (1989) 11 EHRR 175 and *Hussain v UK* 22 EHRR 1 and comments from Judge Morenilla in *Nortier v Netherlands* (1993) 17 EHRR 273: 'minors are entitled to the same protection of their fundamental rights as adults but ... the developing state of their personality – and consequently their limited social responsibility – should be taken into account in applying article 6 of the convention'.
3 Article 6(3)(b).
4 Judgment on 16 December 1999, (2000) *Criminal Law Review* 187.
5 *S v (1) the Principal Reporter and (2) the Lord Advocate* (2001) unreported, Court of Session.
6 R *(on the application of U) v MPC* (2003) 3 All ER 419.
7 Articles 10 and 14.
8 See, eg, rule 7.
9 In rules 1 and 5.
10 Rule 6.
11 Rule 11.
12 Rule 8.
13 Rule 21.
14 Rule 30.
15 R(87)20 adopted at the Committee of Ministers of the Council of Europe on 17 September 1987.
16 Article 40(1).
17 Article 40(2).
18 Article 40(3).
19 Article 40(4).
20 Article 37(3).
21 Article 12.
22 Riyadh Guidelines para 1.1.
23 UN Rules A/RES/45/113, rule 1.
24 Roche, ibid.
25 Ibid.
26 Strang, ibid.
27 Roche, ibid.
28 Available at: www.restorativejustice.org.uk/internl1.html
29 Available at: cm.coe.int/ta/rec/1999/99r19.htm; R(99)19.
30 Council framework decision of 15 March 2001 (2001/220/JHA); (2001) *Official Journal of the European Communities* No 82/1, 22 March.
31 Available at: www.voma.org/docs/ethics.doc
32 United Nations E/CN.15/2002/L.2/Rev.1.
33 *Standards for Restorative Justice*, Restorative Justice Consortium, 2002, available at: www.restorativejustice.org.uk/standard.html

Chapter 4 – Restorative Justice in origin: New Zealand and Australia

The contemporary swing towards restorative justice derives much of its impetus from New Zealand and Australia, where many of the principles referred to in chapter 2 were first articulated and applied. Although we did not visit these countries in the course of our research, their pioneering activities have been so influential that their inclusion is essential in any international review.

New Zealand is well known as the original home of family group conferences developed in response to the increasing political power of the Maori people and at a time when they were successfully reclaiming land and other rights. The push to reform youth justice came from dissatisfaction with the unacceptably high incarceration rates of young Maori and the consequent demand for more culturally appropriate ways of dealing with offending. The community wanted to deal with problems of offending itself, without the heavy arm of the state, while social workers and others were signalling their anxieties over the increasing professionalisation of decisions about child welfare and protection. Reform was therefore 'top-down and bottom-up'[1] and embraced child protection as well as youth offending. It was the first country to provide a statutory basis for conferencing – not only as a means of diversion, but also to provide pre-sentencing advice in serious cases. One of the more dramatic consequences was the immediate closure of the majority of places of detention for young people. More recently, there have been pilot schemes to divert adult offenders from courts and to hold restorative conferences as an aid to sentencing. These initiatives are still fairly new, but it appears that the use of custodial sentences is now falling in the adult Maori community.

The Australian jurisdictions were fairly quick to follow suit and, while they all started with the New Zealand model, they have approached conferencing in different ways. This means that large variation exists in organisation and practice between the two countries and among the Australian states and territories themselves. Kathleen Daly,[2] tells us that 'no other countries in the world have moved as quickly and as completely in embracing the conference idea' and that New Zealand and Australia together have been useful centres of experimentation. She argues that they share a commitment to policies that emphasise social welfare and crime prevention; pride themselves on not following 'the lead' of the United States; and maintain an openness to addressing social problems and to redressing inequalities.[3]

Taken together, all jurisdictions – except two in Australia – have statutory-based schemes, with conferences generally being used as one of a series of possible responses to youth crime. This sustained legislative activity is not typical of developments in other parts of the world and its main objective is to keep young people out of the formal system. We will consider the New Zealand legislation in outline and indicate some of the differences to be found in three Australian jurisdictions: South Australia, the Australian Capital Territory, and New South Wales.

New Zealand
Children, Young Persons and their Families Act 1989

This influential legislation introduced restorative principles and methods to govern both child protection and youth justice practice, drawing on Maori extended family traditions and the principles of the International Convention on the Rights of the Child. It was the culmination of almost a decade of consultation and planning and set out a series of new objectives, including:

- alternatives to criminal proceedings should be used wherever possible;
- measures to deal with offending should aim to strengthen the family/kinship ties and foster their ability to deal with young people;
- youth should be recognised as a mitigating factor;
- sanctions should be the least restrictive possible;
- due regard should be given to the interests of the victim.

In any conflict of principles or interests, the welfare and interests of the young person are to be the deciding factor.

The Act represented a major transfer of power away from the state to family and community groups and an attempt to find family solutions to family problems within the context of the wider community. It is best known for establishing family group conferences but it also formulated a comprehensive system of informal diversion for young people, so that family group conferences are only used for more serious offending.

The new system relied on the Youth Aid division of the police force – established since 1957 – to work with young offenders at the first point of contact. Most young people make admissions to the police, leading to three possible outcomes:

1) in 30 per cent of cases no further action is taken;
2) in about 50 per cent of cases a plan is agreed. This is usually informal: it can be a warning, or involve a home visit or consultation with the school and/or victims. If it is a second or more serious offence the police may order a family group conference to draw up a plan and in this event the case is passed to the youth justice coordinator. Plans often consist of an apology, reparation, community work, residence or specified activities.
3) the 20 per cent of cases at the top of the offending spectrum are sent to court. Roughly half of these will be referred by youth courts to family group conferences, and granted a legal advocate to represent and advise some, and half will be prosecuted because they denied the offence. If they do not deny responsibility it is mandatory for the court to order them to attend a family group conference.

Very serious offences such as rape and grave assaults are the subject of jurisdictional conferences to determine whether they should be tried in the Youth Court or High Court. Murder and manslaughter are automatically tried in the High Court but, even in these cases, where responsibility is not denied, or after conviction, family group conferences will be ordered to inform sentence planning.

Youth justice coordinators
Coordinators are employed by the Department of Social Welfare and often have a social worker background. They have an obligation to promote the Act and to create the optimum environment for its implementation. As well as preparing for conferences, they liaise with police, courts and community, and try to foster inter-agency co-operation. Some coordinators undertake preventive work in schools or to discourage gang culture, and private-sector funding is available for these pursuits in some areas.

Youth courts
Courts deal with 'not guilty' pleas, and order and monitor conferences. Once a conference has taken place, the young person reappears in court for the plan to be presented and agreed, as a form of quality control. Most plans are accepted and, indeed, courts would need to justify non-acceptance. However, if they are too harsh or too lenient, or if a conference has not been sufficiently attended, they may be rejected. In the event of satisfactory completion, the court discharges the young person and the proceedings are deemed never to have commenced. There is no criminal record.

Intervening appearances may be organised where there are difficulties, or if the judge is worried about anything. Generally, the approach is informal, with judges speaking directly to young people and their parents. A Youth Aid Officer will be present, as well as a coordinator and the youth advocate, but there is little adversarial content to proceedings, since there is a statutory duty to put the interests of the young person and family first. This makes for clarity and profoundly affects the part youth advocates play.

Youth advocates

Advocates are attached to youth courts and funded by them, therefore, the question of legal aid does not arise. Advocates are assigned to all cases going to court and will advise and appear for young people. Their function is not to represent in the sense we understand it. They give short explanations as to arrangements in court and have access to the police file. They advise and explain, attend conferences where they have a supportive role and are there as a resource if needed. They may check charges, negotiate appropriate reductions with police and clarify matters, but they do not speak for the young person or family.

Criticisms

Reforms in 1994 picked up on some of the problem areas that had been noted in the first five years since the Act. These reforms discourage arrests without warrant, except in specified circumstances, and insist that young people be told of their rights to legal advice before any questioning by police takes place. There is concern that legal aid is still lacking at this stage.

Although courts oversee the cases they refer to conferences, there is no judicial supervision of the majority of cases that are resolved informally or referred to conferences by police.

Following the original burst of enthusiasm for the potential of the new scheme, it became clear that conferences could not be effective unless the plans they produced were implemented. The consensus supporting the goals and aspirations of the system did not produce sufficient government provision of the necessary resources to achieve them. There were insufficient drug rehabilitation services and anger management courses, meaning that the needs of more serious or persistent offenders in particular were not being met. Appropriate follow-up, like good preparation, is now recognised as being essential. Judge Carruthers, former Principal Youth Court Judge, has said he would like to see the courts given power to direct funding to programmes they consider necessary.

These are significant comments and have encouraged the systematic monitoring that was missing at the inception of the reforms, but the success of the ideas they are based on has been enduring and is visible in the adoption of conferencing in many parts of the world.

Reoffending

Maxwell and Morris,[4] perhaps the best-known academics and commentators in New Zealand, studied a group of young offenders over a period of years. They found that six years after their conferences, more than 40 per cent of young people were not reconvicted, or were convicted once only, and not much more than a quarter were classified as being persistently reconvicted.

They conclude that conferences contribute to lessening the chances of reoffending even when other important factors such as adverse early experiences, other circumstances and subsequent life events are taken into account. They identify the critical factors that make conferences memorable – and therefore presumably effective – for young people. These are:

- not being made to feel a bad person;
- feeling involved in decision-making;
- agreeing with the outcome;
- completing the tasks agreed to;
- feeling sorry;
- meeting the victim;
- apologising; and
- feeling that they had repaired the damage.

They are all factors that reflect key restorative values, processes and outcomes.

Restorative justice for adults

In 1995, three pilot schemes were established to divert selected adult offenders from courts. Judges were to make the relevant decisions at first court appearances and began doing so in 1996. Maxwell and Morris[5] comment that by this time there was considerable support for this move and recognised benefits to the state in making it.

There were three diversionary schemes: Project Turnaround, Te Whanau Awhina, and the Community Accountability Programme, all organised in different ways. Project Turnaround provides a panel of trained community members responsible for developing a plan for each offender. A police officer would also be present, usually the victim, and a coordinator. The goal was to reach a consensual agreement about how the offending should be dealt with and, if the plan was completed, the police would withdraw their evidence. The focus was on reparation to the victim and community.

Te Whanau Awhina was a more specifically Maori programme. The panel here was made up of three or four marae (Maori community) members who would confront the offender and then aim to reintegrate him or her. There were no police present nor any victims. Offenders and victims were not central to the formulation of the plan and, in recognition of this different structure, judges retained greater oversight of these cases. This meant that there could be further court appearances but it preserved the authority of the Maori community, who have a tradition of regulating their own affairs.

The Community Accountability Programme more closely resembled the family group conferences. Victims and offenders made the decisions, within a framework whose objectives were to achieve victim satisfaction and offender accountability.

There are a growing number of further programmes supported and administered by the Crime Prevention Unit and expected to deal with 900 conferences in 2001/2002.[6] Ongoing research will report its findings in due course.

Domestic violence cases are not eligible for diversion, however, other fairly serious and repeat offences are diverted and results are promising. In general, victims have responded well to Project Turnaround and Te Whanau Awhina has been particularly well-accepted by offenders.

Restorative justice conferences for adults are also gaining popularity. They are administered by the Department for Courts and are court-referred restorative processes. In the same way as family group conferences, they rely on victims and offenders (and their supporters) articulating plans to deal with offending. However, they are voluntary – an important distinction – and can only take place if both parties agree. Police, probation and lawyers are invited to attend these events but may choose not to do so.[7] In any event, facilitators provide referring judges with copies of agreements reached and judges will take these into account when sentencing. The idea is to offer victims better outcomes and to reduce reoffending.

Those participating in the pilots were reconvicted less frequently and less seriously than matched controls dealt with in the courts, and those who successfully completed agreements were reconvicted less frequently and seriously than those who did not. The cost benefits noted by Maxwell and Morris[8] are emotional and human (because of diminished reoffending), as well as financial. The Te Whanau Awhani pilot was particularly effective in reducing the number of custodial penalties and thus produced considerable financial savings.

These early findings are valuable, as they indicate that the government's commitment to extending restorative justice to adults is likely to be fruitful, particularly if approached selectively and backed up by resources.

Australia

Six of the eight Australian states and territories have statutory conferencing schemes: New South Wales, the Northern Territory, Queensland, South Australia, Tasmania and Western Australia. The other two: the Australian Capital Territory and Victoria use conferencing, but it is not legislatively based.

John Braithwaite[9] was working on his theory of reintegrative shaming at the same time as the New Zealand system was taking shape. This expounds the idea that offenders are best shamed by those closest to them and that it is the transgressing behaviour, rather than its author, which should be the target of such shaming. This realisation prompted John MacDonald[10] to propose that New Zealand style conferences be adopted, but – in Australia – be located in the police service. This was the background to the inauguration of the Wagga Wagga and similar initiatives, which aimed to provide 'an effective cautioning scheme'[11] run by police. At the same time, there were parliamentary inquiries in a number of states into the perceived problem of increased juvenile offending and how systems might be improved to tackle it.

After some years of intense debate in the early 1990s, the Wagga Wagga model was rejected and most states adopted statutory schemes, as already indicated. However, it is worth mentioning that the Wagga model – in which police facilitate conferences, drawing heavily on the theory of reintegrative shaming – has been used in the United States, Canada and England and Wales. Its legacy has now passed to Thames Valley police, who adopted it when they began conferencing in the UK (see chapter 9).

Statutory conferencing has since become a major feature, at least in some jurisdictions. New South Wales, South Australia and Western Australia run 4,500 to 4,800 youth justice conferences per year between them,[12] although numbers are smaller elsewhere. Unlike New Zealand, where conferencing is used in child protection cases as well, it is primarily applied to youth justice cases in all the Australian jurisdictions.

The Australian jurisdictions had different histories of dealing with youth crime and, indeed, distinct political priorities before the introduction of conferencing. These have influenced the ways in which the schemes have grown so that, for example, Western Australia conferences a high volume of less serious cases, while South Australia favours conferencing for more serious offences (including sexual assaults), and has the highest maximum (300) of community service hours of any state. Equally, arrangements for the coordination of conferences vary, as do the requirements for agreeing outcomes. This part of the world is, therefore, likely to produce some very fruitful research.

South Australia

South Australia was the first Australian state to introduce a legislative scheme (through the Young Offenders Act 1993) and has a respectable tradition of radicalism. Conferences here are almost exclusively a diversion from court, with courts only having a part to play if offenders do not complete their undertakings and the police decide to take breach action. This does not happen often and courts do not approve outcomes as they do in New Zealand.

The South Australian Juvenile Justice (SAJJ) research on conferencing projects has produced some interesting findings in recent years,[13] concentrating both on more violent offences, on those regarded as serious property offences, and looking at the effects of conferences on individuals. It is suggested that in South Australia:

- conferences offer a better experience of procedural justice (fair treatment, being listened to, respected, etc);
- there is relatively less evidence of restorativeness (victim-offender recognition and responsiveness);
- there are limits on offenders' interests in repairing harm and in victims' capacities to see offenders in a positive light;
- victims' anger and fear may be reduced by conferences;
- victims who go to conferences generally feel more positive about offenders over time;
- one year after their conferences, victims felt positive and negative in the same numbers, but were generally satisfied with the way things had been handled and had recovered.

Project director Kathleen Daly's[14] assessment found that about 50 per cent ended on a 'high, positive note of repair and good will' (including ten per cent with very good procedure and skilful coordination) and 50 per cent did not (including 20 per cent mixed good-to-fair and 30 per cent fair-to-poor).

As one would expect, good management of the process often led to better results, although pre-existing attitudes were also linked to success. This study interviewed victims again a year later and found that highly rated conferences were associated with victims' recovery less strongly than before. They did influence victims' attitudes towards offenders, however, a third of victims still thought their offender to be a 'bad' person. Daly argues that although improvement is possible and highly rated conferences do produce more restorative results than those with mixed-to-poor ratings, there are limits to the attainability of good practice, as indicated above.

She is concerned to present restorative justice in a realistic light, arguing that we do it a disservice if we raise expectations of complete success, but acknowledging that reduced reoffending may well emerge as a welcome side-effect. Daly reports that eight to 12 months after their conferences, young people who had participated in highly rated meetings were significantly less likely to be known to reoffend. Significant factors in the reduction of reoffending are remorse and a genuine consensus on the outcome. On the other hand, young men with a history of offending, and who are less integrated, are more likely to reoffend than others.

This suggests that the conduct of conferences may influence future offending, although Daly suspects that the spirit in which young people approach them will dictate the benefits they receive.[15]

The Australian Capital Territory

Conferencing in the ACT has been available for both juveniles and adults for a wide range of offences since the mid-1990s. The Children Services Ordinance 1986 provides a legislative basis for it, but gives no guidance as to how the process should operate. It was masterminded and then extensively evaluated by leading academics and experts at the Australian National University, John Braithwaite and Heather Strang. It is known as the Canberra Reintegrative Shaming Experiments (RISE).

RISE is essentially a large-scale field experiment that compares the effects of courts and conferences. It is designed to test the fairness of conferences; whether recidivism is lower after conferences; and the relative costs. Police conduct conferences and cases are randomly allocated either to them or to the courts. One very significant feature is that RISE has substantial experience in conferencing serious offences.

The research to date indicates[16] that conferences:

- are perceived as fairer than courts (by participants);
- participants feel that they can influence the outcomes;
- there is a helpful perception of being allowed to repay society;
- there is a lower expectation of reoffending;
- victims who attended felt more respected and able to express their views; and
- offenders' respect for police and the law is likely to be increased.

This research includes a survey of young people's offending one year before and one year after committing crimes of violence. Eighty-nine cases and 110 offenders formed the subject of a study, which concluded that conferences reduced reoffending by 38 crimes per 100 offenders. The results were not so good in property crime or in drink-driving, providing evidence that conferencing may be most effectively used in more serious or violent cases.

It is largely the work at RISE that the Metropolitan and Northumbrian police (see chapter 9) are drawing on in the pilot projects now underway in the UK.

New South Wales
Young Offenders Act 1997

This is the most detailed legislation in any Australian jurisdiction, drawing on the United Nation's Convention on the Rights of the Child as well as the New Zealand experience. It enacted a system of diversion, making some changes to the original model to tailor it to local conditions and to incorporate accumulated wisdom. It established a Youth Justice Advisory Committee for ongoing data collection and statistics, review and quality control; specialist (police) youth officers and youth liaison officers to enable smooth administration with conference administrators; and special training for administrators and conveners. Conference administrators were to be local managers and convenors were to be employed on a freelance 'fee for service' basis. It was thought that this would be more appropriate than employing public servants, as in New Zealand, who could not easily be dispensed with.

Police officers were eligible to be convenors, but not as part of their police duties, and their role is as gatekeepers and participants in conferences. The Act stipulates the entitlement to legal advice and gives a ten-day 'cooling off' period for it to be obtained. This was a reaction to the vagueness of the original New Zealand legislation. Lawyers in New South Wales can attend conferences but their role is limited as in New Zealand.

The legislation 'sought to avoid formal intervention in circumstances where young people are naturally likely to desist from crime',[17] but it did not determine who was responsible for funding outcomes and there were only limited funds allocated in each area.

The evaluation in 2000[18] did not specifically mention this and it found that a high percentage of participants were satisfied (although, as commentators[19] have pointed out, it is unclear what satisfaction consists of) with both preparation for conferences and their fairness. The problems it signalled were more to do with time periods and only a minority of conferences were scheduled within the rather limited time specified.

However, there were a number of criticisms and, in particular, participants wanted:

- more appropriate venues;
- more encouragement for victims to attend;
- arresting police officers to attend personally as participants, rather than sending a representative;
- enhanced punctuality, fairness and respect;
- protection of privacy by the nondisclosure of addresses;
- guaranteed neutrality and impartiality;
- more research on the range of appropriate options for outcome plans; and
- more refreshments during conferences.

Another general comment that has been made about the Act is that it is less than adequate on the role and rights of victims.[20] This is no doubt because[21] the history of criminal law jurisprudence, with its emphasis on safeguards against abuse, makes it more difficult to know where victims should belong in criminal procedure. This is pertinent to most other jurisdictions attempting to integrate restorative methods into existing systems.

It is from these beginnings, and the interest and hope they created, that many other international developments sprang. We turn now to look at some variations of the conferencing theme in the United States.

Notes

1 See Daly and Hayes, 'Restorative justice and conferencing', *Handbook of Australian Criminology* (Graycar and Grabosky (eds), 2002).

2 In 'Conferencing in Australia and New Zealand: variations, research findings and prospects', *Restorative Justice for juveniles: conferencing, mediation, and circles'* (Maxwell and Morris (eds), Oxford Hart Publishing).

3 Ibid.

4 See 'Family Group Conferences and Reoffending', *Restorative justice for juveniles'* (Morris and Maxwell (eds), Hart Publishing, 2001).

5 'Restorative Justice for Adult Offenders: the NZ experience', *Repositioning Restorative Justice* (Lode Walgrave (ed), Willan Publishing, 2003).

6 Ibid.

7 Ibid.

8 Ibid.

9 A renowned thinker and advocate of restorative justice, at the Australian National University.

10 Another well-known Australian researcher.

11 Moore and O'Connell: 'Family Conferencing in Wagga Wagga: a communitarian model of justice', *Family Conferencing and Juvenile Justice* (C Alder and J Wundersitz (eds), Australian Institute of Criminology, Canberra, 1994).

12 Daly, 'Conferencing in Australia and New Zealand: variations, research findings and prospects' (see note 2).

13 See Daly and Hayes, 'Restorative Justice And Conferencing', *Handbook of Australian Criminology* (Graycar and Grabosky (eds), Cambridge University Press, 2002).

14 'Making Variation a Virtue: Evaluating the Potential and Limits of Restorative Justice', *Restorative Justice in Context* ' (Weitekamp And Kerner (eds), Willan Publishing, 2003).

15 Daly and Hayes, 'Restorative Justice and Conferencing', *Handbook of Australian Criminology* (Graycar and Grabosky (eds), 2002).

16 H Strang, GC Barnes, J Braithwaite and LW Sherman, *Experiments in Restorative Policing: a Progress Report on the Canberra RISE* (1999).

17 Coumarelos and Weatherburn, 'Targeting Intervention Strategies to Reduce Juvenile Recidivism', *Australia and New Zealand Journal of Criminology* (1995) Vol 34 No 2 pp139–171.

18 Lili Trimboli, *An Evaluation of the New South Wales Youth Justice Conferencing Scheme* (New South Wales Bureau Of Crime Statistics And Research, 2000).

19 Daly and Hayes, 'Restorative Justice and Conferencing', *Australian Handbook of Criminology* (Graycar and Grabosky (eds), 2002).

20 Daly and Hayes, 'Restorative Justice and Conferencing', *Handbook of Australian Criminology* (Graycar and Grabosky (eds), Cambridge University Press, 2002).

21 As Daly tells us in the same chapter.

Chapter 5 – Restorative justice in profusion: the United States

The United States is home to a wealth of restorative justice initiatives and the variation among the different schemes is enormous. We chose to look at Minnesota where restorative practice has been integrated into the criminal justice system – currently being contemplated in England and Wales – and at Texas, whose republican sympathies and conservative policies are interestingly contrasted with innovative work involving the relatives of victims and offenders on death row. This is instructive for different reasons: it provides us with an example of specialised interventions, at a time when we are considering how these may be applied to sensitive cases here.

Restorative initiatives in Minnesota

Minnesota is known for its liberalism and interest in social justice. Here, restorative justice programmes have been established throughout the state by statute[1] and are generally co-ordinated by the Department of Corrections Restorative Justice Initiative. They are sustained by their popularity and, despite the burgeoning prison population throughout the USA, those we spoke to were convinced that this was the way forward. We looked at a selection of programmes across the spectrum, dealing with diversion from court right through to organising circles of support after release from prison.

Woodbury Police Department

The Woodbury Police Department diverts suitable cases to conferences and will also arrange conferences at the request of victims (provided that they are serious enough), even if cases would otherwise have been prosecuted. The only offences that are precluded are life-threatening or sexual assaults and homicides.

Legal advice is available and lawyers may attend conferences but cannot represent their clients in an adversarial sense. If agreements cannot be reached or are not fulfilled within a set time, cases are referred to court. Internal records are kept but offenders do not acquire criminal records.

Twenty-five to 30 per cent of juvenile cases are conferenced and this figure is set to rise to 75 per cent with the recruitment of more staff. Evaluation[2] has shown that re-offending rates for juveniles have fallen from 72.2 per cent to 33.1 per cent. Even repeat offenders' rates have been reduced to 51.8 per cent.

Satisfaction rates for victims (at 85 to 90 per cent), parents (at 82 to 90 per cent) and offenders (at 80 to 85 per cent) have been high. Agreements have been completed on time in 95 per cent of cases and support for police has risen. Conference costs are only 25 per cent of court costs.[3]

Washington County Court program

The Washington County Court Service's Community Justice Program is one example of many victim-offender mediation services and is staffed by volunteer mediators and assisted by community cooperation. Cases are diverted to victim-offender conferencing, small group conferencing or large group conferencing, as appropriate, and all methods are available for both adults and juveniles.

Victim-offender conferences are used in cases where wider participation is not suitable and notifications of resolutions are relayed back to the courts, with which the programme works closely to establish acceptable parameters. Court approval is generally forthcoming.

Small group conferencing includes family and some community participation and may require several mediators. Large group conferences allow large numbers to respond to incidents or offences and are also used preventatively to address community concerns over disputes or anti-social behaviour that could escalate.

Even if a meeting is not considered suitable, victims are given the opportunity to talk about offences, which can be helpful. In one such case, the victim voiced her appreciation, saying:

> This meeting was the best thing that happened since the whole dam thing started! Even if (she) never meets with me, I feel better already just having this meeting with you two. My heart feels better.[4]

The Woodbury Community Conferencing Program (a police initiative) provides a conference service for the Washington programme. Between May 1995 and January 2001, it facilitated 341 conferences: 290 agreements (85 percent) were successfully completed reflecting a wide range of offences. The largest group involved 'juvenile alcohol offenders' (80) and assaults (35). An evaluation found that 100 per cent of victims and 88 per cent of offenders were satisfied with the way their cases had been handled, in comparison with 88 per cent of victims and 61 per cent of offenders whose cases were dealt with directly by the court.[5]

Sentencing circles

The Summit University/Frogtown Community Circle was established in 1998 by Judge Edward Wilson, to tackle crime in this predominantly African-American, economically deprived area of St Paul. Applications are considered from 18- to 35-year-old African-Americans who have committed offences, which attract custody and meet the circle's criteria. Most offences are drug-related and are referred after the first court appearance. The task of the circle is to formulate a sentencing compact that must be ratified by the judge. Defence attorneys attend but their role is primarily advisory.

Preparation is crucial and the compact will involve remaining drug-free and possibly staying in stable housing, continuing with education, seeking employment, and undertaking community work. The continuing support offered by circle members is key to the fulfilment of compacts and the need for this has been considerable in many cases.

Post-sentence initiatives

Community justice programmes

Community justice programmes offer mediation during prison sentences and courts make specific referrals as part of the sentence. They are popular and we were immediately given an example involving a woman who had been kicked in the head, hospitalised and suffered memory loss. She discovered, during mediation, that her assailant had been brought up in a violent background and told him that he could make amends by starting life afresh, bringing his own child up differently and breaking the cycle of violence. In the longer term, he had managed this successfully.

Juvenile probation

The Restorative Justice Unit of the juvenile probation department provides victim-offender mediation and family group conferencing for all types of offences. While staff in Minneapolis acknowledge that not all cases are suitable for these interventions, they nevertheless claim success in some difficult and intractable cases and try to approach them in an individualised, flexible way.

They had found domestic assaults by juveniles – often as part of a long and complex history of family dysfunction – particularly challenging and in 2000 started a family rebuilding programme, 'relative care conferencing', based on a slightly different approach. This aimed to mobilise support and obtain information from the wider family, so that facilitators could work with families to produce contracts within the six-month adjournments given by the courts.

Probation officers monitor progress and longer term support is available if necessary. If the terms of contracts are substantially met, cases are dismissed.

There are specific programmes for serious offences and evidence, confirming wider evaluations,[6] testifies to their efficacy. We heard about one such intervention, following the sexual assault and murder of a young Cambodian Hmong girl, whose body was dumped in a public park. One of the defendants, Jenny, desperately wanted to apologise to the victim's family for her part in the offence and after considerable preparation, the girl's family agreed to her meeting their therapist. They wanted her to know about their loss and their community and to give her the chance to make some form of amends. Jenny's remorse was obvious and this was conveyed to the family, together with her letter of apology. She was symbolically forgiven, giving her hope that she would be able to resume her own life later on. The family appreciated her remorse and apology.

Prison

Minnesota imprisons fewer people than many other states and there are a variety of restorative programmes in custodial establishments, involving community service, victim empathy or victim impact panels.[7] The more intensive programmes offer victim-offender mediation or assist in the creation of ongoing circles of support (by family, friends and supporters).

At the Shakopee facility for women, victim empathy sessions are available to all and community service projects and other agencies provide programmes before and after release. Women have access to cognitive behavioural programmes, to help them develop skills in problem-solving, negotiating and handling emotions and relationships. Individual mentors work with community organisations to facilitate reintegration and the general response among staff to these interventions has been very positive.

There is no doubt that victim empathy has increased and women appreciate the chance to give something back to the community. Behaviour improves with the requirement of cognitive skills and victim advocacy groups have reported more positive views of the correctional system, enhancing the likelihood of successful reintegration.

Minnesota Correctional Facility Red Wing, near Minneapolis, committed itself to restorative processes in 2000, by declaring that its aims were to restore offender, victim and community, and to promote public safety and offender accountability.

Staff have now been trained and residents (serious, violent young offenders aged between 12 and 20) may participate in cognitive behavioural and victim empathy classes. There is a wealth of community service projects on offer. Victim impact panels and circles are popular, teaching problem-solving techniques, encouraging the making of amends and helping with the transition back to society. There are also specialised sex-offender and chemical dependency treatments.

Conferences can be arranged as appropriate and these can be large: including family members, friends, teachers, probation officers and others, as well as victims and their supporters. Preparation with both parties was said to be extensive and often includes establishing an ongoing 'community' of support.

We heard about a number of cases in which conferences were able to provide a human context for the events that had occurred, enabling anxiety to be relieved, unexpected links to be found and reintegration promoted.

Conferences take place in the young person's home area, in order to maximise support. So far, no one has tried to escape, although young people are understandably anxious about their reception. Many have had numerous previous chances, but without sufficient incentives or support, they have not broken the cycle of offending. Community conferencing intends to do this and we were given an example of its success in the case of a young man who had caused serious damage to a community centre, without being able to see that there had been any human victims. At the conference he heard of the many activities – including a lunch club for the elderly – that were carried out there. He was able to recognise that they would suffer while the centre was repaired. He agreed to spend time with them and, while this was intended to help him appreciate the consequences of the damage in more depth, it also made it clear to those who had been affected that he was just an ordinary young man, who now bitterly regretted his actions.

A plan of action for the offender's return to his neighbourhood is agreed in every case and there are regular meetings until the parole period expires. At that point, there is a party to celebrate and to welcome him home.[8]

Restorative justice with girls and young women
Restorative practice has been found to be especially effective with girls and young women in custody. There were only six of them in August 2002 and, after trying the model developed with adolescent boys at Red Wing Correctional Facility with

them, it became clear that a different emphasis was needed. Research showed that the young women defined themselves and solved their problems primarily through their connections to other people. Their needs were therefore relationship-based and their offending frequently resulted in institutionalisation and estrangement from their families and communities, compounding their problems. These findings led to the creation of more tailored programmes.

Circles of support were organised to bring together family and community members, with the first one being planned as soon as the young woman arrives. Meetings continue regularly during sentences, furloughs[9] and probation and aim to tackle difficult and painful issues in a supportive and constructive setting. The DOC Planner for Female Offenders described how young women who believe that they had alienated their entire family are frequently overwhelmed on entering a room full of people prepared to try to help. Professionals have also discovered that (as with child protection in New Zealand) rather than identifying the difficulties themselves, they need to listen to the young women and their families, and then discuss what might be needed.

They have learned that young women may find it hard to acknowledge the harm they have done to themselves and often they are victims of physical, sexual or emotional abuse. If this can be recognised, it is often the first step to addressing other problems and to moving away from offending.

We were told the story of Priscilla, one young resident whose behaviour had been so disturbed and antisocial that it had finally put her into custody. Her background was violent and abusive and complicated by alcohol and drug abuse. However, with the help of the restorative justice co-ordinator, Priscilla identified the important relationships in her life that needed to be rebuilt. Five circles were subsequently held, attended by her family, friends and others. They discussed the issues, expressed their care and concern and planned for the future. Most importantly, she was able to talk to her abuser and he was able to apologise and discuss the steps he was taking to address his own problems. At another circle, Priscilla explained to her drug-using friends that she would not be able to associate with them if their drug use continued. These sessions also led her to accept help with her relationships and chemical dependency that she had previously refused.

Restorative initiatives in Texas

Texas is known for its huge prison population (over 163,000) and its extensive and controversial use of the death penalty,[10] but it is nevertheless host to a number of trailblazing restorative programmes, which are supported financially by the state. These tend to be locally organised and victims' groups have played an especially important part leading to the Department of Criminal Justice establishing victim-offender mediation in a range of cases, including the most serious.

Community justice

Ronald Earle, a district attorney based in Austin, adopted the idea of community justice in the mid-1980s in order to try to find more creative solutions to crime. There is now a galaxy of programmes aimed at reducing crime and at building a more law-abiding and safer society. He insists that restorative justice is far tougher for offenders, as it involves a true emotional encounter with the people they have harmed.

He cites the example of a drunk driver who caused severe injuries to a passenger in another car. She was still in pain after 30 or 40 operations and when she began to describe the impact the crash had had on her, at the sentencing circle they both attended, she poured three bags of prescribed drugs onto the floor. As she related details of her life since the accident, the offender had to leave the room twice because he was so horrified at the devastating consequences of his behaviour.

Neighbourhood Conference Committees are a means of dealing with cases diverted from court by prosecutors. In suitable cases, a committee of four or five trained volunteers from the community will meet a panel of local people to discuss the circumstances and agree on an appropriate sanction. This may involve direct reparation, apologies, or community service and will be monitored by a panel member. Earle would like young people to be included in these panels, to provide a peer response, and he believes that programmes like these strengthen community identity.

Community impact panels were set up specifically for use in drugs cases, where there is often high recidivism, and are offered to those who are given 18-month to two-year sentences. Panels include neighbours, social workers, police officers and friends or relatives, and are arranged at the beginning and end of the sentence. They discuss what is needed to help them give up drugs and what is available to them in prison to help them make more of their lives upon release. Support may be offered to families during the sentence but, as the programme is still new, it is too early to know how effective it is. The district attorney's office insists that its impact is heightened by community involvement and reports that both offenders and police have responded positively.

Victim-offender mediation and dialogue in crimes of severe violence
Background

The Victim Services Division pioneered mediation in the most serious cases, by establishing a victim-offender mediation/dialogue programme, run by a professional coordinator, but largely staffed by trained volunteers. They take on a relatively small number of cases – five or six per month – and continually recruit more volunteers. There is a rigorous training programme, of about 70 hours in total, and once volunteers start working they must do 24 hours further training each year. This is because mediation in such a context requires especially sensitive and lengthy preparation. Mark Umbreit, a leading expert at the University of Minnesota, tells us that these are special circumstances:[11] there is greater emotional intensity and an absolute need for non-judgemental attitudes in very challenging circumstances. This means that the programme is expensive (just under $1,000 per case), but the state recognises its quality.

The programme provides victims of violent crime (whether survivors or relatives) with the opportunity to take part in a structured face-to-face meeting with 'their' offender, at their request. Often this happens many years after the offence, when people feel ready to communicate and need to do so in order to move on. One example concerns Linda White, who contacted the programme 15 years after her daughter was raped and murdered. Mediation was arranged with one of the offenders, the other two were not deemed suitable, and Linda and her granddaughter were able to explain what the last 15 years had been like for them, and to ask detailed questions. The programme has found that details, which often only the offender can know, are frequently very important to victims. It was inevitably highly emotional for all of them, but beneficial.

Victims must make contact with the programme themselves. If offenders participate, which they often do, they gain no practical benefit in terms of parole or execution. If they are unwilling or unsuitable, victims may prepare statements – in writing or on video – to describe the impact of the offence. The making of these statements is liberating in itself, although offenders cannot, of course, be forced to receive them. For example, a 21-year-old victim of physical and sexual abuse recorded a video statement to her stepfather, the perpetrator, as his release date approached. He refused to see it, but she clearly valued the opportunity to describe her feelings, to make clear that she held him responsible and to tell him she wanted no further contact with him.

Alternatively, victims can be offered surrogate mediation with an offender who has committed a similar crime. While this cannot take the place of direct mediation, it provides the victim with the opportunity to relay experiences and fears.

Where participation is agreed, mediators hope to be able to prepare for a meeting in about six months' time. They encourage victims to go through their life stories and to make sure that they have good emotional support throughout the period. They work on recognising and articulating strong emotion, in preparation for managing the meeting and the feelings it will bring up. Mediators give examples of possible reactions on both sides and discuss offenders' backgrounds in general terms. The day before the meeting, they give particular attention to trying to minimise the impact of any possible shocks or surprises.

Offenders similarly receive careful preparation. Mediators have to be certain that they will not do or say anything inappropriate or damaging during the meeting and offenders have their own difficulties. They are often very fearful, ashamed, guilty and depressed. It is important that they are also supported and they are encouraged to use special arrangements talk to families, friends and chaplains, as well as the mediator.

Evaluation has shown that mediation is often extremely positive: victims have felt more able to move on with their lives afterwards and hearing offenders take responsibility often lifts burdens of guilt, as many feel partly responsible themselves. The coordinator has witnessed the transformative effect on some participants, so that even some measure of forgiveness may sometimes be possible.

Follow-up sessions, after such cathartic events, are essential. Mediators offer 90 days of debriefing and both parties receive a copy of any agreement on the anniversary of the meeting, which may be accompanied by a visit. Follow-up could be indefinite but, in practice, people have to be referred elsewhere. Participants often become strong advocates for the programme, some eventually training as mediators.

While offenders are almost always in custody and many are on death row, occasionally, mediations take place while the offender is on probation. In one case, involving a drunk driver who had killed four young children, an intervention was ordered by the court. All parties were keen to participate and so, in that sense, it could still be seen as voluntary, with the court simply endorsing the general will. The judge ordered that the sentence should include giving presentations on the danger of drinking and driving to a series of local schools. The offender was extremely anxious about doing this but, as part of the affirmation agreement, the victims' mother offered to accompany and support him during these visits, which was recognised as being valuable to them all.

Evaluation

In the year July 2002 to June 2003, the programme provided a service for 172 victims. These involved the following cases:

- five causing death by driving while under the influence of drugs or alcohol;
- 19 adult sexual assault;
- 24 child sexual abuse;
- 92 murder;
- six robbery;
- nine assault;
- 17 other.

Thirty-three mediations were completed during this period. Evaluation has shown that virtually all victims who have participated in these programmes have found them beneficial. A doctor, whose sister had been killed by a drunk driver commented:

> *I couldn't begin to heal until I let go of my hatred … after the mediation I felt a great sense of relief … I was now ready to find enjoyment in life again.*

A teacher, who was assaulted and nearly killed, stated:

> *It helped me end this ordeal … for me, it has made a difference in my life, though this type of meeting is not for everyone.*

An offender, who met with the mother of a man he had killed, commented:

> *It felt good to be able to bring her some relief and to express my remorse to her.*[12]

Mediation has clearly helped some people immeasurably. It is the quality of their experiences, which ensures that demand for the service continues to grow, even if it is not suitable for everyone.

Notes

1 Minnesota Statute chapter 611A.775 restorative justice programmes. Available at: www.revisor.leg.state.mn.us/stats/611A/775.html

2 D Hines, *Woodbury Police Department Community Restorative Conference Program Recidivism Study* (available form Woodbury County Police Department, Minnesota, 2000).

3 Woodbury police data from 1997 showed an average conference to cost $120, compared with an average court case of $536.

4 J Shirts (ed), *Washington County Community Justice Program* Newsletter, Vol 2 No 1, p3.

5 M Umbreit and C Fercello, *Client Evaluation of the Victim/Offender Conference Program in Washington County* (Center for Restorative Justice and Peacemaking, University of Minnesota, St Paul, 1997).

6 M Umbreit, W Bradshaw and R Coates, *Victim-sensitive Offender Dialogue in Crimes of Severe Violence: differing needs, approaches and implications* (Center for Restorative Justice and Peacemaking, University of Minnesota, St Paul, 2001).

7 Victim-impact panels involve victims explaining the impact of offending to offenders, who have not directly offended against them.

8 John Braithwaite has suggested that there should be a formal ceremony to mark offenders' reintegration into law-abiding society. See J Braithwaite, *Crime, Shame and Reintegration* (Cambridge University Press, 1989).

9 'Furlough' describes the phase of a custodial sentence when the offender has been released from custody, but could be recalled if he violates the conditions of the release.

10 There have been 305 executions in Texas since 1976. Thirty-three executions took place in 2002 (information from the Death Penalty Information Center, available at www.deathpenaltyinfo.org/dpicresults.php?find=texas&x=27&y=20.

11 M Umbreit, W Bradshaw and R Coates, *Victim-sensitive Offender Dialogue in Crimes of Severe Violence: differing needs, approaches and implications* (Centre for Restorative Justice and Peacemaking, University of Minnesota, St Paul, 2001).

12 Ibid, p13.

Chapter 6 – Restorative justice in institutionalised settings: Austria and Norway

Victim-offender mediation in Europe is already fairly established. It is most often used as a form of diversion from courts, in what are generally inquisitorial systems. However, it is now being extended to adults and used both before and after sentence. We chose to look at Austria, a system run by professionals, where mediation for juveniles was started as long ago as 1985, and at Norway, where it is used more widely, almost as a philosophy of life, where community involvement is especially important.

Austria
Background
Austria had, for many years, allowed for some diversion from prosecution for adults if they showed 'active repentance', while the juvenile justice system continued to operate on the principle of mandatory prosecution. Because sentencing alternatives were few, numbers in detention rose unacceptably, leading to a widespread demand for change among the professionals running the system: prosecutors, judges, lawyers and probation officers. Reform came in the shape of the victim-offender mediation pilot projects established in 1985, given legislative effect by the Juvenile Justice Act 1988 (itself a reflection of their success) and also as a result of the thinking expounded in the Beijing Rules (see chapter 3). The subsequent extension of victim-offender mediation to adults and to more serious offences testifies to the acceptance of conflict resolution as a method of approach, and embedded it firmly into the criminal justice system.

The pilot projects
The first pilot project, involving juveniles (aged 14 to 18), was established in Salzburg in 1984, followed by pilots in Vienna and Linz in 1985.[1] There had been extensive consultation beforehand and their way of working was enshrined in the Juvenile Justice Act 1988 and applied nationwide.

The system in operation
The Act introduced a wide range of diversionary options for young people: non-prosecution, mediation, compensation, probation and community service, with the consequence that most minor first offences were dismissed.

Section 6 of the Act obliges the prosecution to discontinue where certain criteria are met:

- if the penalty would be a prison sentence of not more than five years; or
- if the penalty would be financial; or
- if no penalty would be imposed (ie, the court would absolutely discharge) and if further measures are not required to prevent the offender from committing further offences.

The young person must admit responsibility and be prepared to compensate for the consequences of the offence to the best of his/her ability in order to qualify for discontinuance.

Section 7 of the Act allows courts to discontinue cases in line with these criteria. Section 8 enables courts to refer cases to mediation, following an application by either the offender or the victim, so long as the offence is not serious and punishment is not necessary to prevent offending. Section 9 enables courts to discontinue cases provisionally: they can do this if the facts are clear, if the matter is not serious and if punishment is not required to prevent further offending. Conditions will be attached, often featuring a probationary period of up to two years and discontinuance will be finalised when the period of time has elapsed or the conditions are fulfilled.

Criminal records
There has been a significant reduction in criminal records as a result of these provisions. Only those who are convicted by the courts have a record. Discontinued cases and out-of-court settlements are recorded for police purposes only, in case of any future offending. They are not for court use and the resulting avoidance of labelling and stigma is thought to assist in the prevention of reoffending.

The diversion process
Police report all juvenile cases to the public prosecutor, who has discretion to dismiss the case completely, refer it to the probation/mediation service or prosecute. As we have seen, courts may also refer cases to mediation. These case referrals will be assigned to a specially trained probation officer, who works only as a mediator.

The ATA

The ATA is a special 'out-of-court conflict resolution unit' (Aussergerlichtlicher Tatausleich). Although funded by the Ministry of Justice, ATA is an autonomous body for mediators. All members have relevant qualifications, often in social work or psychology, and are well trained in both the theoretical and practical aspects of mediation. Standards are high and the ongoing dialogue with academic research aims to ensure that the work is informed by a coherent philosophy. Staff are expected to adhere to ATA's overall ethos, derived from the educational and conflict resolution aspirations of the legislation. ATA staff meet regularly with judges and prosecutors to discuss their work and this helps maintain the confidence of the courts.

Mediation

Preparation of both parties is taken very seriously. This assists the mediator and participants in working through the reconciliation meetings that follow, helping to move towards realistic plans and concentrating on quality solutions rather than speed. If the offender is willing to undertake mediation and make reparation but the victim declines, the courts may still be told that the intervention has been satisfactory and the case may be dismissed. The victim's decision whether to take part in mediation therefore does not influence the outcome of the case.

Indirect mediation is also on offer and is used most commonly in property offences, where victims are less likely to need to resolve their feelings. Nevertheless, direct exchange is regarded as being more productive and victims' willingness to attend may be helped by the perception that this option is less daunting than going to court for judicial questioning. In the context of an investigatory court system, such as in Austria, this would be the alternative if the case were prosecuted. Public confidence in mediation presumably also promotes cooperation.

There has been a gradual move to mediate more serious offences, particularly offences of violence. This is a response to the finding that mediation may help to identify underlying causes in these cases more effectively than, for example, in cases of dishonesty. It has also become clear that less serious cases may not require this level of resources or dialogue and can be appropriately dealt with by dismissal or discontinuance.

The role of lawyers

Legal advice is available to participants in mediation free of charge and is commonly taken in relation to levels of compensation during the preparatory phase. If agreements are worked out and accepted in principle, one or both lawyers might attend the subsequent meeting (mediation will often involve a number of meetings), where the actual amount and terms of reparation are fixed.

Essentially, the role of the lawyer is to advise, consult and facilitate. It is not to provide representation as in an adversarial system. In any event, this would defeat the object of the exercise. Austria's court system is inquisitorial and the role of lawyers is somewhat different. It is accepted that victims may have independent legal advice within such a system.

Adults
The popularity of the new juvenile system very soon led to pressure to extend it to adults. Pilot projects were set up in 1992 and enjoyed similar success, although the numbers being referred were not quite as high. Practice led the way, as it had done in 1985, and the Criminal Procedural Law Amendment Act 1999 enshrined this in legislation. The arrangements mirror those already in place for juveniles, the only difference being that young people may be diverted on more than one occasion, whereas adults are not likely to have more than one chance.

Domestic violence
The women's refuge movement was originally opposed to out-of-court settlements in cases of domestic violence. They argued that violent men needed to be publicly condemned and that mediation could not provide such a function, even though courts had not been noticeably successful in achieving results. However, the Ministry of Justice did not want to specify exclusions in the legislation and relied on the success of the pilot projects to carry its point.

Research[2] undertaken on the 25 to 30 per cent of cases involving domestic violence in the pilot projects revealed that, although mediation did not necessarily achieve any greater improvement in behaviour, it nevertheless helped women to articulate and discuss these problems, which had a strengthening effect. The ATA, conscious of the potential imbalance of power in these cases, developed a specialised response. It allocated two mediators: one male and one female, to try to ensure support for the weaker party. It also provided some ongoing supervision by requiring participants to report back on any changes that occurred. Cases were screened with great care, in the knowledge that some cases would be better dealt with by other means and that it was vital mediation retained its credibility.

Evaluation

Continuing evaluation is an important characteristic of the system, built in at inception. It is thought this has encouraged high levels of victim participation and satisfaction.[3] Ninety-six per cent of victims in juvenile cases have participated and successful resolutions have been achieved in 75 per cent of cases. Eighty-five per cent of victims and offenders in adult cases were prepared to participate, resulting in mediation in 72 per cent. Direct mediation was found to be more successful and a recent study[4] showed 'high or very high' levels of satisfaction among 83 per cent of participants. The same study indicated high levels of satisfaction among women in domestic violence cases. In general, the perception was that men who attended mediation were more likely to accept responsibility for their actions, although women admitted to uneasiness during the course of the meeting.

In 2001, 26 per cent of cases were diverted from prosecution. Of these, just under 20 per cent were referred to mediation[5] and 2.8 per cent of cases resulted in unconditional prison sentences. ATA statistics for 2001 show that 9,000 referrals were received, with just over 25 per cent of these being juvenile cases. Half of these and a third of the adult cases were described as 'situational': stemming from a quarrel or assault in a public place and resulting in physical injury. Twenty-six per cent involved domestic conflicts between partners; ten per cent disputes with close family or other relatives; 16 per cent disputes with known social connections; and ten per cent entailed school, workplace and neighbourhood conflicts.

Sixty-one per cent of adult cases ended in agreement, 30 per cent failed (and went back to court) and in nine per cent of cases, the parties failed to attend or mediation did not occur for some other reason. Victims were unwilling to co-operate in only one per cent of cases. Seventy-eight per cent of juvenile cases resulted in agreement, 15 per cent failed to reach an agreement, and mediation did not occur in seven per cent of cases, sometimes because another diversionary measure was recommended instead.

Research[6] conducted over a three-year period, using data from 1993 and 1994, suggests that victim-offender mediation has a positive impact upon rates of recidivism. For first offenders, reoffending among the sample who had participated in mediation was less than half that of the control group. For offenders with previous convictions, reoffending among the mediation group was still approximately two-thirds that of the control group.

Norway

The influential Norwegian criminologist, Nils Christie, published his seminal 'Conflicts as Property' article in 1977. In it, he argued that conflicts had been stolen from the people by an increasingly professionalised response by the system. He maintained that the ability to resolve disputes at an individual and community level is an important aspect of civil society, which should reflect the wishes of its citizens. He questioned the extent to which prison should be allowed to expand because of society's inability to deal with its own problems and, two years later, a government report responded by suggesting mediation as a viable response to juvenile offending. This report, informed and supported by Christie's thinking, inspired the establishment of a nationwide framework for mediation services.

The Municipal Mediation Boards Act 1991 inaugurated this framework by the introduction of mediation boards to 'mediate in disputes which arise as a result of one or more persons causing loss or damage or other offences against a third party'. In practice, this is an impressively wide-ranging remit. Cases can be referred by prosecutors, judges, housing and social welfare departments and almost any other individual or government department. Many people refer their own disputes to the boards: evidence of an underlying belief in the importance of community decision-making articulated by Nils Christie. This philosophy has meant that mediation has developed with the use of volunteer mediators and representatives of the community, facilitating the resolution of local conflicts.

Every municipality has access to a mediation board (or service) and these provide a means to resolve conflicts in both the criminal and civil spheres. In criminal cases, mediation is available at four different stages:

- as an alternative to prosecution for adults and young people over the age of 15 (the age of criminal responsibility in Norway);
- for young people under 15;
- as a condition of a suspended prison sentence;
- as part of a community punishment.

The Criminal Procedures Act 1998 gives prosecutors the discretion to refer cases to mediation. A circular[7] issued by the Director General of Public Prosecutions in 1993 recommends mediation for younger offenders and more minor offences, such as, criminal damage, dishonesty and car theft. The Ministry of Justice, however, is keen to extend its use to more serious offences and the Director General has agreed that mediation may be appropriate in violent cases where there is a conflict, but supports deterrent sentences in cases of severe violence. Even in these instances, judges may partially opt to suspend the defendant's sentence on condition that he undertakes mediation, especially where there will be future contact between the parties.

Mediation as a diversionary measure

Prosecutors, who are expected to suggest sentences to courts, may also divert all cases that would not attract immediate custody. The majority of cases in the Moss police district just south of Oslo that were diverted in 2001 involved damaged property, assaults and a small number of burglaries. Apparently, violence had increased and the Norwegian approach, as articulated by Nils Christie, favours mediation in neighbourhood disputes and in instances where there has been a history of conflict. These are guiding principles and, for practical purposes, victims must be identifiable and the police must indicate that there is some likelihood of agreement being reached.

Four hundred and nineteen cases were mediated in Ostfold (south of Oslo) in 2001, 90 per cent of those were referred. Once agreements are fulfilled, the prosecutor closes the case and no criminal record results, although an administrative record is kept. Interestingly, domestic violence and racial harassment cases will generally go to court, as they are regarded as being too serious, or intractable for mediation.

Mediation in cases involving under-15-year-olds

Under-15-year-olds may not be prosecuted in Norway but police can ask the parties whether they would like to enter mediation and, if so, can transfer their cases to the mediation board. This is purely voluntary, although parents must also agree. However, there are no consequences for the young people if they choose not to participate. Many in fact do, because of the belief in its efficacy.

Mediation as part of a sentence

Mediation has been very little used in this context: only about 20 cases (since the 1998 Act) up until September 2002. This is surprising because prosecutors, who after all are responsible for diverting cases, could suggest the inclusion of mediation as a condition of a suspended sentence to judges. If mediation is so ordered and either the agreement is not fulfilled or it does not take place, the court may review the sentence. Currently, the Ministry of Justice is proposing new legislation to promote the greater use of mediation with suspended sentences.

Mediation as part of a community penalty

The community penalty was introduced in 2002 and includes a range of programmes intended to promote behavioural change. Sentences range from 30 to 420 hours of community punishment and, if mediation is to be a part of the overall package, the probation and mediation services will cooperate in organising it. Joint training sessions have been arranged to enhance such cooperation: necessary because the probation service has tended to work mainly as a law enforcement agency and has relatively little experience of restorative approaches. Discussions are ongoing but preparation is possibly not taken as seriously in Norway as in other places. However, the parties are screened for suitability and offenders with serious mental health or drug abuse problems are generally excluded.

Mediation practice

Direct mediation is the only intervention on offer in Norway. Participants may be accompanied by a supporter but not by a legal representative, for the usual reasons. Parents or guardians of children under 18 years need to agree and have a right to attend. Mediators stress their impartiality. Any unbalancing factor – such as manipulation, racism, discrimination or dominance – that jeopardises a fair agreement, results in the case being sent back to the prosecutor.

All agreements are recorded in writing and either party can retract within a week of the agreement's approval. The parties report back to the mediation service once the conditions of the agreement have been fulfilled, whereupon the co-ordinator files a further report with the prosecutor. If the agreement is breached, the coordinator must also be informed and mediation may be renewed if circumstances have rendered it unrealistic.

Each mediation service has a coordinator, employed by the host municipality and a pool of volunteer mediators, who are paid a small fee (approx £10 per hour) plus expenses. There should be at least one mediator in every municipality and Oslo, the largest city, has over 100.

The principle of community involvement and the use of volunteer – as opposed to professional – mediators is central to the philosophy of the mediation service. This means that it is particularly important that mediators are representative of the community as a whole and, wherever possible, they will be matched with parties from similar backgrounds. However, practice does not live up to theory. White, middle-class volunteers remain predominant but the service is conscious that a diverse and changing group of mediators are necessary to avoid stagnation and rigidity. This remains their aim.

Mediation training

Mediation training – and its ongoing availability – has been of variable quality. It was hoped that, by making the Ministry of Justice responsible in November 2002, this would improve. So far, a new training module based on experiential learning has been introduced and a new training council will now meet regularly to organise, evaluate and update training. Advanced and specialised training will be provided for those who are more experienced, for new co-ordinators, and for those dealing with cases of more serious violence. The training council must guarantee the quality of mediation nationally. The Ministry of Justice is responsible for finance, practice and procedure, and professional supervision and training, while the municipalities are responsible for administration. Many municipalities have offered insufficient support to the services and the structure is currently under review. It looks as though the Ministry of Justice will have overall control in future, despite the considerable pressure for greater community involvement. The result is that the mediation service is likely to be streamlined so that there will be one service per county, as opposed to the 40 services for 19 counties at present.

Ostfold Mediation Service

We visited the mediation service in the county of Ostfold, south of Oslo. Ostfold has a population of 250,000 and contains 19 municipalities and one police district with three police offices. The mediation service serves the entire county and its referrals come from the usual wide range of sources. It is considerably smaller than Oslo and it seems that less attention is paid here to preparing for mediation. For example, separate meetings with the participants are not usually arranged prior to mediation unless there is a high degree of conflict and mediation itself will usually only be one session.

In 2001, approximately 85 per cent of referrals resulted in mediation. Eighty per cent of these cases reached agreement. Of these, 94 per cent of agreements were successfully fulfilled. Four hundred and seventy nine offenders participated: 40 per cent of the total caseload. Sixty-eight per cent of these were between 15 and 17 and 80 per cent were under 24 years of age. The majority of cases involved damage to property, but there were also violent offences, burglaries and a few cases of shoplifting. There were only a few neighbour disputes but cases entailing more serious violence increased. One case we were told about involved one young man stabbing another in the thigh, necessitating 16 stitches. The prosecutor had referred it because of the obvious remorse of the defendant, and it had been successful.

Another successful referral was an ongoing conflict between Norwegian and Macedonian neighbours, which had led to the Norwegian tearing down his neighbour's hedge on four occasions and repeatedly threatening him. When he insulted his wife, the Macedonian finally went to the police to complain of harassment and was referred to mediation, at the end of which the Norwegian apologised. During the dialogue, many resentments were expressed: the Norwegian was not fully literate and was not working because of a heart condition. He was envious of his neighbour's house and car and believed that he had an easy life in Norway as an immigrant. The Macedonian explained that he had achieved this by working hard at two jobs. They both agreed that they should have talked to one another before the situation had escalated and they agreed to communicate with one another more reasonably in the future.

The co-ordinator here has found it easy to recruit volunteer mediators, although they are insufficiently representative of the community. There are currently 25 of them, who have all attended a three-day training course on communication skills and understanding and handling interpersonal conflicts. Regular quarterly meetings are held, so that mediators can discuss their work with each other and they are subject to a two-year probationary period. Some have been working since 1993, when the service was set up, and this is controversial. In Nils Christie's terms, they might be thought to approach the professionalisation that he thought should be discouraged.

Coordinators also meet regularly and there is an ongoing dialogue with the police to keep them informed of practice and to encourage them to extend the range of cases referred.

Evaluation

The Ministry of Justice's statistics for 2001 show that 6,134 criminal cases were referred to mediation, of which 4,811 resulted in agreements fulfilled within that year. Nearly 40 per cent of these involved property crimes, mostly thefts and a small number of burglaries. Twenty-three per cent involved criminal damage. Fifteen per cent involved crimes categorised as violence, bullying and menace. The remainder mostly entailed family and neighbour disputes. Seventy-nine per cent of agreements were fulfilled, 16 per cent remained current at the time the statistics were compiled and 4.5 per cent had been broken. A very small percentage was renegotiated. Forty-one per cent of agreements comprised financial compensation, 21 per cent comprised reparations whether direct or indirect, while seven per cent comprised a combination of the two. Twenty-one per cent of agreements involved reconciliation. Other types of agreement were reached in the remaining ten per cent of cases. An earlier evaluation of mediation had found that 98 per cent of offenders and 95 per cent of victims or complainants were sufficiently satisfied with the process to recommend it to others.

In 1996, the Ministry of Justice funded Oslo University's Institute of Criminology to evaluate qualitative aspects of the mediation service.[8] Over 90 per cent of victims stated that they would recommend mediation as a means of resolving conflicts. Recidivism has not been evaluated.

Notes

1 C Pelikan, 'Victim offender mediation in Austria', *European Forum for Victim Offender Mediation and Restorative Justice* (ed) (*Victim Offender Mediation in Europe*, Leuven University Press, Belgium, 2000).

2 Ibid.

3 Ibid.

4 A Altweger and E Hintzl, 'Consumer Satisfaction of Injured Parties in VOM in Innsbruck'.

5 Ibid.

6 Cited by David Miers, 'An International Evaluation of Restorative Justice', 2002.

7 Circular Part 11 Vol 2, 1993.

8 S Kemeny, 'Policy Developments and the Concept of Restorative Justice Through Mediation', *European Forum for Victim Offender Mediation and Restorative Justice* (ed) (*Victim Offender Mediation in Europe*, Leuven University Press, Belgium, 2000), pp83–98.

Chapter 7 – Restorative Justice in Northern Ireland and Scotland

Northern Ireland
The development of a statutory system

The Review of the Criminal Justice System in Northern Ireland was an essential part of the ongoing peace process. Reforms to courts and the legal system, indissolubly linked with political interests, were recognised as priorities. Throughout the years of conflict there had been many victims and the need to acknowledge their grievances was urgent. It was equally important to find other ways of steering young people away from offending in a changing society. Taken together, these factors argued for a new beginning: to find a way forward in keeping with the vision of a more cohesive society and to adhere to the human rights principles put forward as the cornerstone of its achievement.

This was the background to the very significant recommendation of the review to adopt a system of family group conferences for young offenders and victims, based on diversion by both prosecutors and the courts, where guilt is accepted. This is the New Zealand system (described in chapter 4) with some variations. It is the first attempt within the UK to mainstream conferencing. The Justice (Northern Ireland) Act 2002 (implementing the recommendation) provides that all offences, save those triable on indictment only, and those attracting life imprisonment, are to be diverted in this way.

As in New Zealand and Australia, the participants at conferences will produce plans to be approved by the courts and legal representatives, who may act as advisers, should be specially trained for the new system.

This is a major move forward, and could be a pointer to the future in other parts of the UK. It is a clean sheet, drawing on international human rights standards and experience; a move away from the community-based initiatives, which have made great contributions at grassroots level but have been lacking in wider support.

It is too early to comment further on the new scheme but we did visit some community projects, forged out of the historically divided background and perceived illegitimacy of the courts and police. This was the situation that led to 'community' policing by both loyalist and republican paramilitaries. Punishment beatings and shootings were a main feature and RUC statistics show that between 1973 and 2000, approximately 2,300 people may have been the victims of punishment shootings and 1,700 of punishment beatings. Many more had been exiled. While there is a debate about the accuracy of the statistics, there is no doubt about the level of violence these practices involved.

From the beginning, the Northern Ireland office distanced itself from these new approaches. It maintained that it could not support programmes, which do not engage with the existing system, and signalled concerns about human rights in a context where there was a high-level of coercion.

The development of community-based restorative initiatives

Kieran McEvoy and Harry Mika, academics who have been closely involved with the projects,[1] repeat that the rationale behind punishment violence is the mistrust and hostility of the RUC by republicans and the frustration at the state's inability to deal with the IRA by loyalists. This led to each side feeling driven to defend its own community.

This position was reviewed in the late 1990s, as the peace process moved towards the Good Friday Agreement. It became clear that continuing violence was a hindrance to political aspirations on both sides and this prompted a concerted move to try to control it by a coalition of local communities, organisations and academics. It was also accepted that punishment beatings and shootings were ineffective: joy-riders who had been shot in the knees were often not deterred and would be stealing cars (on crutches) again within days of discharge from hospital.

There was also mounting concern about the effects on children who had known only violence and trauma and the necessity to break this cycle in the interests of a peaceful future. Nevertheless, paramilitaries still faced pressure to deal with offending and it took time for non-violent methods to be accepted in the pilot projects.

Greater Shankill Alternatives

Greater Shankill Alternatives was established in the loyalist area of Woodvale in 1998, to deal with young people involved in persistent criminal and anti-social behaviour – many of whom would previously have been subject to punishment violence, threats or exclusion.

NIACRO (Northern Ireland Association for the Care and Rehabilitation of Offenders) commissioned Tom Winstone, an ex-paramilitary prisoner, to undertake some preparatory research and a diverse steering group was established. This included representatives from the council, churches, youth groups and EPIC (the Ex-Prisoners Interpretative Centre, a UVF ex-prisoners group). The UDA and police declined to be involved but the UVF supports the project, provided that it does not intervene in inter-factional disputes, internal disciplinary matters, drug-related or sex offences. What it offers is intensive work for a small group and a preventative programme for larger numbers.

Harry Mika's recent evaluation[2] showed that between 1998 and 2001, 129 formal referrals or inquiries were received. Ninety per cent of these were under threat from the paramilitaries at the time of referral and cases included:

- theft (31 per cent);
- criminal damage or arson (21 per cent);
- car theft (18 per cent); and
- disruptive behaviour/assault at home or school (seven per cent).

Referrals came from paramilitary organisations themselves (42 per cent), community sources (27 per cent), social services (18 per cent) and self-referrals or referrals from NIACRO (seven per cent). Paramilitary violence has reduced from 17 cases in the eight months prior to the launch of Alternatives in 1998, to only three cases in the successive four years.

Most referrals were young men aged between ten and 18 and about half attended the intensive programme (available to 20 young people per year). Programmes, tailored to the individual's specific needs, generally last from seven to ten months. There are daily individual sessions with the support worker and the participants are encouraged to examine the impact of their behaviour.

Initial assessment is critical. Some young people are too damaged to engage constructively with the programme immediately and they will be offered support or counselling until they are ready to take an active part. Mediation is on offer when appropriate and has been fairly successful, producing appropriate agreements and identifying resources to back them up.

According to the evaluation, 86 per cent of young people agreed contracts within a month of referral and 64 per cent of these were completed within six months. The project includes practical help in finding employment or reparative work and it also negotiates with educational authorities and drug rehabilitation, counselling and other relevant agencies.

Alternatives employs a few professional staff but is largely staffed by volunteers. There are 12 trained volunteer youth workers and 19 trained volunteer mediators, all of whom live or work locally. The manager, Debbie Watters, attributes their success to the intensity of the programme and to local support and commitment. She is adamant that statutory services cannot meet peoples' needs in the same way and that this is reflected in their lesser success.

There is no doubt that Alternatives has gained community approval. The following comments – provided by a project to foster debate about these questions – indicate the general endorsement of the programme:[3]

> *My son was in trouble and came to Alternatives and went on the programme and it completely changed him. It learned him to respect other people and their property. He's no angel, but he's completely changed.*

> *We had a young person who came through Alternatives, we were asked if he had any work he could do ... he worked his guts out cleaning the blackest smoke out of all our closets. I mean, the place was a mess, but he worked hard. And it was interesting to see how other people coming in and out of the centre reacted to him. It changed people's views about kids who get involved in joyriding; they saw him as a person. So unknowingly he was educating other people.*

The project believes that community development and recovery will grow as more people both train as mediators and have positive experiences of mediation. Watters is convinced of the benefits of participating in solutions for all those involved.

Four further projects are due to start in the near future, based in East and North Belfast, Bangor and Armagh. Training is currently underway and Alternatives has provided a useful model.

Community Restorative Justice Ireland

Community Restorative Justice Ireland (CRJI) is a similar response to republican punishment violence. It started with a group of community members, academics and youth workers working with the IRA towards adopting a non-violent response to crime and anti-social behaviour. It was based on community consultation and academic research and produced a community-based model of conflict resolution. Four pilot projects, three in Belfast and one in Derry, were established on the most deprived and crime-ridden estates. Within three years,

700 local people had participated in an accredited training programme in mediation.

Referrals come from paramilitary organisations, housing, social services, probation departments and, increasingly, direct from individuals. Jim Auld, the project manager, told us that people valued the confidentiality and humane treatment that the scheme offered.

Most cases go either to mediation or to conferences and agreements are followed up three and six months later. CRJI also negotiates with the paramilitaries to arrange the return and reintegration of people who have previously been exiled. This is rarely objected to in the current climate and it is agreed that the project should be informed of any recidivism so that timely interventions are possible.

CRJI will not deal with offences of murder, rape or sexual abuse (the latter are referred to the social services department) but they deal with most other offences and disputes, including the aftermath of serious crime.

We were given a typical example, of a middle-aged man ('Donal'), who had lived in the same area all his life. He had a good relationship with his neighbours and his family lived in the surrounding streets. When the neighbours went abroad, leaving their two teenage sons at home, they and their friends went on a drinking spree and, finally, in search of more alcohol, broke into Donal's house. They inflicted multiple stab wounds and set his house on fire. When they were arrested, other neighbours picketed their homes in protest and one of Donal's brothers, a paramilitary, fired shots through one of the assailant's windows. The boys' families were devastated both by their behaviour and by the breakdown in community relationships.

Mediators were able to help justifiably outraged neighbours to see that the offenders' families had also suffered. It took many months for Donal's family to say that they did not blame their neighbours for the actions of their sons but, finally, they were able to do this in a genuine way, so that community feeling could be restored. Auld pointed out that the formal system would have been inadequate in tackling these wider conflicts and divisions.

Evaluation

Mika's evaluation[4] of CRJI focused on 508 cases between 1999 and 2001. Cases generally involved assaults and property crimes; neighbourhood and family conflict; and youth at risk. One hundred and fifteen cases (23 per cent) featured paramilitary violence. A significant proportion was fairly serious but in the majority that went to mediation or conferences, 93 per cent were successfully resolved and the figure was 89 per cent for indirectly mediated cases. CRJI's objectives have expanded over the three-year evaluation period, from dealing purely with casework, to developing a proactive role to promote community safety.

Resources

These programmes have experienced serious resource problems. Funding has been uncertain and sporadic, affecting not only the retention of project managers and administrators but also the essential pool of trained volunteers, which has reduced considerably. The amount of work that can be taken on, as well as its quality, is inevitably compromised.

Auld would like a relationship with the formal system, as this would boost credibility and make funding easier but, at the same time, he regards it as limited and would not wish to be bound by traditional ideas. He fears that this would result in the project being marginalised and only able to deal with minor cases, rather than exploring its potential to respond to serious offences and issues.

Both projects would like to improve their relationships with statutory services and with the police. Links have already been forged with social services, probation and the youth service but police may still have lingering suspicions that they may be fronts for paramilitary activity. This is largely a thing of the past; however, the Northern Ireland office remains sceptical.

The recent Review of the Criminal Justice System found that there was a role for community restorative justice, providing that it did not become involved in investigating crimes, that it forged proper links with police and other criminal justice agencies and ensured due process. While the government has obviously accepted restorative processes in the form of the new statutory scheme, it is still not willing to support schemes outside the existing criminal justice system, fearing that these initiatives may not be able to maintain impartiality and a balance of power.

Scotland

Prosecutors in Scotland – procurator fiscals – have more powers than the CPS. They have long diverted cases from prosecution to social work, mental health, alcohol abuse and other interventions. They can also impose fines. The Stewart Committee Report in 1983[5] confirmed the benefits of this approach for adults.

For young people, the Children's Hearings, established under the Social Work (Scotland) Act 1968, provided a less formal, more child-centred way of dealing with offending or child protection. The hearings rely on a non-punitive philosophy and aim to meet individual needs and circumstances in a creative, flexible and problem-solving framework. Despite insufficient resources in some areas for effective social work follow-up, the hearings have wide support from within the system and have doubtless influenced the thinking of the Scottish Executive, which, in 2002, began to fund restorative programmes.

SACRO (the Scottish Association for the Care and Resettlement of Offenders) is the source of many of these programmes and, indeed, has run such initiatives for over 15 years, giving them the necessary basis from which to expand. Its Youth Justice Services now offer conferencing (most often family group conferencing), direct and indirect mediation and victim awareness (or empathy) programmes.

They are open to nine- to 17-year-olds, who have been charged with a recent (no more than three months old) offence and who are referred by reporters (officers, usually lawyers, who act as gatekeepers for Children's Hearings). Families, police, social services or other agencies can also make referrals, providing that reporters have been consulted. Priority is given to cases involving the greatest impact on victims[6] but sexual offences, offences against the police, road traffic and documentation, and drugs offences are not usually considered suitable.

If programmes are successful, cases are discharged. Otherwise, they may be referred for hearing and this will happen anyway if there are welfare concerns. SACRO categorises young people as either situational or persistent offenders. The situational offenders are likely to grow out of their behaviour but persistent offenders, a much smaller group, commit a disproportionate number of offences. They come, overwhelmingly, from chaotic and difficult backgrounds and present particular challenges. Restorative interventions for them need to be more intensive and require more resources. However, SACRO maintains that if they can be prepared sufficiently to participate constructively in a programme, this can have a powerful effect.

Adults

The majority of adult cases are referred by way of fiscal diversion. However, referrals can also be made after conviction and before sentence. The Stewart Committee Report advocated diversion in the latter instance, so that outcomes could be taken into account by sentencers. We were quoted a recent case, in which the victim of a serious assault wanted to meet the four young women responsible for it. They responded positively in the meeting (arranged by SACRO), were obviously shocked at the consequences of their actions and keen to make amends. The court recognised this by giving them probation orders and the sheriff announced that, but for their participation, they would have received custodial sentences. This is reminiscent of the recent decision by our own Court of Appeal (see chapter 3). SACRO is currently training mediators to work in prisons, to expand their work further in a society where the percentage of people in prison is very high.

Volunteers and the role of the community

SACRO uses volunteer mediators, enabling greater access to mediation but also expressing a commitment to community involvement, which is one of their main values. As in Norway, mediators are matched with participants from similar neighbourhood and backgrounds, with a community interest in resolving such matters. It is thought that volunteers will gradually disseminate the restorative ethos and it is hoped that this will gradually change attitudes and improve community safety.

SACRO has found that restorative processes are most likely to be successful in more serious cases, such as robbery or assault, where the impact upon the victim has been significant. If these victims will participate, their contributions are likely to have a greater effect upon the young person and victims may benefit more from the process because of their correspondingly more intense need to resolve their feelings. However, SACRO does believe that victims and offenders may also derive benefit in more minor cases.

Notes

1 K McEvoy and H Mika, 'Punishment, Policing and Praxis: restorative justice and non-violent alternatives to paramilitary punishments in Northern Ireland', *Policing and Society* (2001), Vol 11, pp359–382.
2 H Mika, *Evaluation: Greater Shankil Alternatives* (2002).
3 M Hall, 'Farset Community Think-tank Project', *Restoring Relationships: a community exploration of anti-social behaviour, punishment beatings and restorative justice* (Island Publications, County Antrim, 2000).
4 H Mika, 'The Role of Community Restorative Justice', *Making our Communities Safe for the Future* (CRJI).
5 *Kilbrandon Report: Children and Young Persons* (Cmnd 2306, HMSO, 1964).
6 SACRO's *Youth Justice Services document*, Appendix 1, Index for severity of victim impact.

Chapter 8 – Youth justice in England and Wales

The statutory context
The Crime and Disorder Act 1998

The government's 1997 election manifesto included a commitment to deal quickly with young offenders, at a time when there was a groundswell of dissatisfaction with the system and a political consensus that it needed reform. The changes that followed have been wide-ranging and have created a new infrastructure, landscape and language of youth justice. They have generally commanded all-party support.

The Crime and Disorder Act 1998 was the first indication of the government's growing interest in restorative methods and victims' rights. It introduced Youth Offending Teams (YOTs) to coordinate services and make plans for their provision and funding (s39). Local authorities were obliged to establish YOTs, in consultation with police, probation and health and education authorities, who would all be represented to form a multi-agency team.

Section 37 makes the principal aim of the legislation to prevent offending. Government guidance suggested that this should be achieved by:

- the swift administration of justice;
- the confronting of young offenders with the consequences of their actions;
- tackling particular factors identified in individual cases;
- punishment proportionate to the seriousness and persistence of the offending;
- encouraging reparation; and
- reinforcing parental responsibility.

The work of the YOTs was to be infused by the three principles of responsibility, restoration and reintegration.

Youth courts were given the power to make action plan orders (Powers of Criminal Courts (Sentencing) Act 2000 ss69–72) and reparation orders (PCC(S)A 2000 ss73–75) to assist in achieving these ends. Action plan orders may be imposed on suitable ten- to 17-year-olds and involve supervision with various conditions attached, so that they are tailored closely to the defendant's circumstances. They must include reparation. Reparation orders are similarly applicable and consist of an order to make specific reparation (not more than 24 hours, to be completed within three months). The plethora of other youth court orders remains, but the availability of new services means that the opportunity to include reparative elements into their content is there.

The Act also set up an independent Youth Justice Board (YJB) (s41(5)):

- to monitor and provide for youth justice services;
- to advise the Home Secretary;
- to set national standards and provide custodial accommodation;
- to advise on how the principal aim – to prevent offending – might be most effectively achieved; and
- to identify, promote and make grants for the development of good practice.

The YJB is responsible for the juvenile secure estate and for commissioning research. It funds a wide range of youth work and keeps full statistics. Crime And Disorder Act 1998 ss38 to 39 give it a duty to ensure the availability of appropriate youth justice services and, again, police, probation and health authorities have a duty to co-operate with them.

These services include:

- prevention and early intervention;
- the provision of appropriate adults;
- assessment and intervention work in relation to final warnings (see below);
- support on bail;
- placement in local authority accommodation of those remanded by the courts;
- the provision of reports and of responsible officers to organise parenting, child safety, reparation and action plan orders;
- the supervision of community sentences;
- post-release supervision; and
- the implementation of referral orders (see below).

Reprimand and final warnings replace cautions as responses to first and second brushes with the law respectively. Final warnings trigger referrals to the YOTs and, therefore, interventions. These are not convictions but may be citable in any subsequent court proceedings.

Youth Justice and Criminal Evidence Act 1999
The Youth Justice And Criminal Evidence Act 1999 explicitly endorsed restorative principles for the first time. The sections dealing with referral orders (now found in PCC(S)A 2000 ss16–28) represent a huge shift in thinking and a courageous attempt to be 'tough on the causes of crime'. All young offenders pleading guilty for the first time in the youth courts were to be referred to Youth Offender Panels (YOPs), unless they were to be sentenced to custody or absolutely discharged. Panels were to be established by the YOTs, to consist of three members: one from the YOT and two selected volunteers with different skills and experience, who would be trained to meet with young people and work out a contract to deal with the significant factors identified during the meeting. The idea was to achieve uniformity by giving every young person the chance to participate in this way, in relatively informal circumstances.

Courts making referral orders must therefore make it clear that these require attendance at panel meetings, agreeing such a contract (to promote the acceptance of responsibility, reparation and reintegration) with the panel and abiding by its terms. Referral orders can last from three to 12 months and, if there is a failure at any stage, defendants can be referred back to the original court for sentence. Associated offences – which are common and have often had the effect of delaying proceedings – may be dealt with by way of concurrent referral orders and may not be the subject of other types of community disposal. This is to avoid a multiplicity of sentences (the subject of much criticism) and to concentrate efforts on preventing offending.

Young people are encouraged to bring their parents (and courts must order at least one appropriate person to attend if they are under 16). They may also choose to bring someone who has a good influence on them. It is hoped that victims will attend, although so far their participation has been low.

Panels usually hold review meetings after one month to discuss progress and then every three months for the duration of contract. The terms of the agreement may be varied if circumstances change and when a contract is completed the conviction is regarded as 'spent' for the purposes of the Rehabilitation of Offenders Act 1974. This is not the equivalent of having no criminal record, but it is a considerable improvement and, in practice, many parents are relieved.

Legal representation

Legal representation is not available for panel meetings, although young people will usually be represented at the court hearing when the referral is made. They will, therefore, have access to legal advice before the admission of guilt is made. The thinking behind this is familiar. It is feared that lawyers, in their traditional role as representatives, will hinder direct communication with the young people and between parties.

However, following the European Court decision in *V and T v UK* and the subsequent *Lanark* case (see chapter 3), if the young person is not able to participate effectively because of youth or psychological, emotional, intellectual or behavioural difficulties, an application for legal representation may have to be granted. The Court of Session (in the *Lanark* case) found that Children's Panels in Scotland had the discretion to grant such representation. There has so far been no challenge in England and Wales, but it is possible that there may be, and the youth offender panels must, by implication, have similar discretion.

The JUSTICE research

JUSTICE set out to get a bird's eye view of the ways in which YOTs were implementing the legislation and to highlight the advantages and disadvantages that they were encountering. The study involved ten teams: nine Youth Offending Teams (Barnet, Camden, Ealing, Enfield, Hammersmith and Fulham, Haringey, Nottinghamshire, Wandsworth and Westminster) and the MARS (Mediation and Reparation Service) project (run by Crime Concern and attached to South West Hampshire YOT). MARS had been selected to pilot reparation and action plan orders and Nottinghamshire, Hammersmith and Fulham, and Westminster subsequently piloted referral orders (as well as reparation and action plan orders). Our survey was selective and impressionistic, aimed at getting a general idea of evolving practice in a fast-changing environment. Unfortunately, we were not able to observe any panels, but we did speak to numerous YOT and community panel members in London and also contacted YOTs in Wales and other parts of England. We found that their comments and experience were similar.

Each team is organised slightly differently in terms of personnel (and who performs what role) and partnership arrangements with, for example, mediation services. Significantly, some are better resourced than others, putting them ahead in important areas such as preparation and programmes to follow up any problems identified. While generally following Youth Justice Board guidance, each team has developed an individual approach. For some, restorative work is central, for others, it is yet another new initiative to be managed as well as resources allow.

Participation

In many areas, the Data Protection Act 1998 was interpreted as meaning that police had to make the first contact with victims because they were not permitted to pass on contact details. This had an adverse effect on participation because police were often not trained for this function and did not understand the importance and sensitivity of preparation. However, there were places, such as Hampshire where MARS operates, where the Act was not regarded as precluding project workers from contacting victims first, and local police apparently accepted this. The latter interpretation greatly enhanced victim involvement.

This stumbling block was quickly recognised and the Association of Chief Police Officers has now issued guidance requiring consent from victims to share their data with YOTs and relevant agencies on an 'opt out' basis. If they do not opt out, they will be approached directly by the team responsible, sometimes by way of 'opt-out' appointments, and this strategy is said to have paid dividends. Participation is demonstrably, and logically, increased by personal visits, as opposed to telephone contact only.

Victims are offered a range of options:

- simple discussion (with the worker responsible) of the offence and its consequences;
- shuttle mediation;
- direct mediation or conferencing; or
- the preparation of a statement/video that can be used in lieu of their presence.

Experience shows that it may take three to four weeks to prepare victims for direct mediation. In line with accepted principles, pressure must never be applied. We were told that working with victims was, in any event, not possible until offenders had been assessed as suitable. Although it was a process that could not be rushed, it was nevertheless desirable that face-to-face contact occurred relatively soon after the offence in order to get the most benefit from its impact.

Court time-scales are not yet adjusted to these requirements and allow little time for any restorative work to be agreed. Similarly, youth offender panels should meet within 20 days of a referral order being made. However, actual meetings with victims may take place only at review meetings if victims feel unable to attend on the first occasion or where the offenders need to undertake victim empathy work.

Victims should be offered further support after mediation or conferencing but, in most teams, this was necessarily limited to two or three months, after which a referral could be made to Victim Support or an appropriate counselling agency.

Young people and their families need as much preparation for meetings as victims do and it has already been remarked that some young people found it difficult to speak among a group of adults, potentially prejudicing their participation and the quality of the meeting. Others were articulate and seemed genuinely to have thought about the effects of their behaviour. It appears that parents were generally satisfied that they and their children were treated fairly, that agreements were reasonable, and that help had been forthcoming.

Where victims attend, they are only present for part of the meeting and are asked to leave during any confidential discussions of offenders' backgrounds and circumstances. So far, it seems that both YOT workers and victims have behaved sensitively and respectfully in this regard.

The YOT perspective

All teams had some observations in common. They agreed that victims mostly appreciated the opportunity to be listened to and many were pleased for their views to be communicated to offenders. Some wanted to discuss possible reparation and all were glad of information about the progress and outcome of the case.

Many teams have found that this is the extent of the majority of victims' involvement. An early evaluation of referral orders[1] confirmed that victim involvement had been lower than expected and far below that achieved in some other countries.[2] Victims attended panel meetings in only 13 per cent of cases for which there was an identifiable victim.[3]

At Camden YOT, where direct participation is relatively high, victim contact is undertaken by two police officers attached to the team, who estimate that they spend 80 per cent of their time visiting, talking to and supporting victims. Enfield YOT has a partnership with AMENDS, a local mediation agency, whose coordinator trains and supervises a team of volunteer mediators. Without their assistance, it would not be possible to offer the level of support that is essential to achieve the high level (60 per cent) of victim participation.

Referral orders

Referral orders have only been in operation nationally since April 2002. Our research indicated that the recruitment of the panel members had, generally speaking, been fairly successful. Inevitably, some are more representative of the local community than others, however, all teams had been impressed by their reliability and commitment and their increasing confidence.

Nevertheless, there were some criticisms. Because referral orders were mandatory, some very minor offences, such as fare evasion or minor public order matters, were caught up in the system. This was perceived as unnecessary and disproportionate and possibly counter-productive. It raised questions about the dangers of net-widening and one team estimated that approximately 75 per cent of those who appeared before panels would previously have been dealt with by way of conditional discharges and would have been unlikely to reoffend.

Panels, and subsequently YOTs, have frequently struggled to devise suitable contracts for young people who receive referral orders for lesser offences. Some panels have been very creative. In Westminster, for instance, a boy convicted of cannabis possession was asked to research drugs charities, make a donation to one and return to explain his choice to the panel. Referral orders cannot be discharged early for good progress and one coordinator commented that an initial positive experience could soon become negative, especially if it involved taking time off work or out of education. National standards, requiring a minimum amount of contact during the course of the order, are regarded as inflexible.

There was also a concern that young people receiving a first conviction for a more serious offence may be treated more harshly than someone who had previous convictions and was therefore not subject to a referral order. The evidence as to the extent of this problem is unclear and the YJB are currently considering it.

Finally, referral orders are costly. The evaluation of the pilot schemes estimated an average cost of £690.[4] One manager in the JUSTICE study estimated that they cost his team approximately £1,000 and, in many minor cases, this was not regarded as a good use of resources.

The government has reacted speedily – perhaps because of YJB lobbying – to amend referral orders (by virtue of SI 2003 No1605) as from 18 August 2003. They are now discretionary for non-imprisonable offences (such as fare evasion), mitigating some of the criticism but not resolving the issue completely, as many very minor offences (for example, theft of a pint of milk) are imprisonable.

Reconviction rates

There has been some research into the effect of the new orders on reconviction rates but it is difficult to find studies that are recent, large-scale and over a long enough period of time to produce convincing results. A recent Home Office study[5] showed a reconviction rate of 51.2 per cent for juvenile males subject to a reparation order (compared to 66.6 per cent for supervision orders, 52.8 per cent for action plan orders and 69.2 per cent for community rehabilitation orders).[6] Oxfordshire YOT requires all young people receiving a final warning to participate in some form of restorative activity. This approach has seen a reduction of 18.8 per cent in reconviction rates over one year.[7]

Notes

1 T Newburn et al, *The Introduction of Referral Orders into the Youth Justice System: final report* (Home Office Research Study 242, Research Development and Statistics Directorate, Communication Development Unit, 2002), pp41–52.

2 A Morris, G Maxwell and J Robertson 'Giving Victims a Voice: a New Zealand experiment', *Howard Journal* (1993) 32(4), pp304–321; H Strang, G Barnes, J Braithwaite and L Sherman, *Experiments in Restorative Policing: a progress report on the Canberra reintegrative shaming experiments* (RISE, Canberra, ANU, 1999), both cited in Newburn et al, *The Introduction of Referral Orders into the Youth Justice System: final report* (Home Office Research Study 242, Research Development and Statistics Directorate Communication Development Unit, 2002) pp41–52.

3 T Newburn et al, *The Introduction of Referral Orders into the Youth Justice System: final report* (Home Office Research Study 242, Research Development and Statistics Directorate, Communication Development Unit, 2002), p41.

4 Ibid, p58.

5 See *Restorative Justice: the government's strategy* (Home Office, 22 July 2003).

6 One-year juvenile reconviction rates (Home Office online publication 18/03).

7 *Restorative Justice: the government's strategy* (Home Office, 22 July 2003).

Chapter 9 – Non-statutory provision: adults and the police in England and Wales

This chapter deals with the use of restorative justice in England and Wales in relation to adults. This has, hitherto, been conducted on a non-statutory basis. The ideas and the practice of restorative justice have enthused many of those engaged in the criminal justice process within the non-government sector, the prisons and the police. In particular, the Thames Valley Police have done much to promote restorative practice by their imaginative adoption of restorative cautioning. Its commitment to integrating these methods into police and preventative work (in schools and elsewhere) has ensured the attention of politicians, already attracted to new ideas about improving victims' services and political profile. The Thames Valley Police have had a major influence on policy and it is unlikely that the government's strategy to mainstream restorative justice would have been formulated without their efforts.

Thames Valley Police Restorative Cautioning Initiative

Restorative cautioning and conferencing were piloted in Aylesbury in 1997 and have been in operation in all 11 Thames Valley Police areas since 1998 for adults as well as young people. This initiative was inspired by the example of New South Wales, where police conferences were introduced not only to encourage young people to take responsibility for their actions but also to improve (faltering) police relationships with the young community. Such restorative work draws upon John Braithwaite's theory of re-integrative shaming:[1] that society's support for wrongdoers as people, combined with disapproval of their behaviour, is effective in reducing offending. In this new version of cautioning, victims are invited to police stations for the event. If a victim attends, the process is known as a restorative conference, if not, a restorative caution. In either case, police officers facilitate meetings using scripted questions designed to find expression both for emotions and for a description of the consequences of what has happened. The aims are the usual ones of responsibility, reparation and reintegration.

As one might expect, the 2002 evaluation of this new scheme[2] was mixed. On the positive side, the cautioning exercise was thought to have improved overall. The participants were mostly satisfied and outcomes were reasonable. Both parties valued the opportunity to meet and to express themselves. They thought, on the whole, that the aims were met and almost a third of offenders entered into written reparation agreements (most of the others apologised), which were completed within a year. Importantly, restorative cautioning appeared to be more effective. Comparative studies of young offenders, aged ten to 17, indicated that those who had received restorative cautions were only half as likely to be re-sanctioned within a year.

On the negative side, the evaluation revealed evidence of a significant number of cases of poor quality facilitation, under-preparation of parties and coercion of offenders or their supporters. In some cases, cautions had even been given without an admission of guilt, although this did improve during the course of the study. Over a third of the participants were not contacted directly by the facilitator before the cautioning session, so that there was virtually no preparation and they were confused as to the purpose of the meeting. Nearly two-fifths of offenders stated that the meeting made them feel like a bad person – a result the process was specifically meant to avoid. The authors suggested that the danger of net-widening could increase as police became more enthusiastic about the benefits of restorative cautioning. The study further commented on the possibility of relationships with the police deteriorating if people admitted guilt and opted for a caution/conference rather than being tried and acquitted in court. Lastly, it was suggested that the public needed a better understanding of offenders and offending.

These, or other, criticisms were to be expected in an area where experience of this approach was so limited. It is clear that accumulating learning is already changing attitudes and practice. However, policymakers have seized on the promising opportunity presented to them by the Thames Valley experiments. The Criminal Justice Act 2003 provides for conditional cautioning, that is, allowing police, working with the CPS, to give offenders cautions for first-time or minor offences with conditions attached. Conditions will have to be for rehabilitative or reparative purposes. The offender must accept these and may be prosecuted if the conditions are not met.

Bourne End Restorative Justice Unit

Bourne End provides restorative conferencing for young people as part of their caution. When we visited, it was dealing with about 20 cases per week and officers had been impressed by how positive and powerful conferences could be. Despite insufficient resources for proper preparation in all cases, it appeared that some participants – usually different family members – were able to take advantage of this opportunity to communicate in a wider setting. Conferences were reported to have been particularly valuable in otherwise intractable cases such as neighbour disputes and harassment. Victims had been attending in more than half of all cases but police were aware of the importance of a flexible approach and shuttle mediation was sometimes used. This had been found to be an effective alternative.

We observed two restorative cautions, both of which revealed there is still a great deal to learn about conference preparation and implementation. It was perhaps indicative of the generally low level of victim participation that the victims were not present in either case. The first case involved a 17-year-old, accused of allowing himself to be carried in a stolen vehicle and theft of milk from doorsteps. He attended the session alone, as his chosen supporter was his co-defendant. The facilitator told him that the victim was elderly and encouraged the offender to see things from the point of view of the victim. The young man expressed remorse and said he would not have been involved if he had known the circumstances. There was further discussion dealing with his feelings about the episode and how he might change his behaviour in the future. When it was made clear to him that amends would have to be made, he suggested writing a letter of apology.

The second case involved four 15-year-olds who were arrested for being found on enclosed premises, namely a disused school building. Additionally, one had been accused of criminal damage to a light switch and another of possession of cannabis. All attended with their parents. It was unclear whether any of them believed they had actually done anything wrong and the boy accused of criminal damage specifically denied it.

These cautions were not representative and we were undoubtedly unlucky not to see a conference at which a victim participated. We felt that the dynamics would have been significantly altered by the presence of a victim and police officers involved all agreed how valuable this was. Nevertheless, each case contained elements of some concern. The young man in the first case should not have been alone. This contradicts the aims and purposes of this kind of cautioning, which are specifically to involve families or other supporters. Although he did express remorse, it was difficult to assess its long-term effect in the absence of any family or other participants to witness the event. The second case was even more problematic. It was not clear that the young people accepted they had done very much wrong by entering abandoned premises, while bored in the school holidays. Some at least may have had a defence and the group did not appear to have had legal advice.

Our observations confirmed some of the findings of the research. We know that, as a result, training and awareness have been improved. But our two random examples illustrate the need for standards, accountability and continual concern for the value of the process. They also point to the advisability of a comprehensive system of diversion (for example, as in Austria) with options other than mediation and conferencing. Conditional cautions may help to develop these.

The role of the police

Restorative cautioning is now being adopted by other police services: Nottinghamshire, West Mercia, Dyfed and Powys among them. Thames Valley's trailblazing start is having its effect and much thought has been given to training, preparation and follow-up in order to improve standards and learn from accumulated experience. Similar steps are being taken in Scotland and in other parts of the world. Police forces themselves express a growing interest in restorative justice as a way of developing community policing. They have extended these principles to preventative work in schools and communities, workplace conflicts, antisocial behaviour and to the resolution of complaints against police.

However, there are different views about the appropriateness of police continuing to conduct conferences, as opposed to cautions or crime prevention work, in the longer term. The main objection is that, for justice to be seen to be done, the appearance of independence and impartiality is fundamental. No matter how skilled or well-trained police facilitators are, it will be hard for them to be perceived as neutral participants, particularly if they are in uniform and if conferences are conducted in police stations. The police, as a service, have overall responsibilities to investigate crime, to detect offenders, to initiate prosecutions and to act on behalf of victims. A number of commentators[3] argue that these undermine the notion of impartiality, which is essential in a process that must maintain – and be seen to maintain – an equal balance between the parties if it is to achieve its aims.

It is further suggested that if meetings are convened in police stations, it is hard to see how officers can avoid dominating proceedings on their own territory. Furthermore, accountability is likely to be compromised: offenders, and maybe victims too, are likely to see the police as running the show. The evaluation of Thames Valley Police[4] implicitly confirmed this in its finding that inappropriate police behaviour was unchallenged in conferences. Others have queried how any criticisms of treatment by the police – by victims, witnesses or offenders – can be properly canvassed when police colleagues are facilitating. These are contradictions that may be impossible to resolve in every case and fairness may be affected.

On the other hand, supporters of police facilitation point to the benefit to police themselves in changing attitudes and the development of restorative policing in the future. They refer to the opportunity it gives the community to scrutinise their work and to the reassurance that police can offer victims, who may be more prepared to attend police-organised conferences. There is research (by Strang and McCold)[5] showing that participants in such conferences feel that they have been treated as fairly as, or more fairly than, in other conferences or in courts. The Home Office funded projects in the Metropolitan and Northumbrian police areas (see chapter 8) involve police-facilitated events. These draw on experience from the RISE project in Canberra and on the expertise of Heather Strang, an eminent theorist and practitioner, who advocates these arrangements.

We have already noted the spread of restorative cautioning and the interest in restorative policing generally. As far as conferencing is concerned, however, it is noteworthy that police in New South Wales no longer (since the Young Offenders Act 1997) act as convenors in their official capacity but attend conferences as participants only. This legislation gave police an important gate-keeping role and the discretion to divert in a number of ways – including cautions – in which their involvement was central. Nevertheless, it was decided that they would only be able to convene conferences in a freelance, off-duty capacity, in the same way as other professionals (see chapter 4).

The police, particularly Thames Valley Police, have undoubtedly been the driving force behind much change. They have acted on the perception that victims' needs have been neglected and have responded constructively to the diminished public confidence in the criminal justice system. They should certainly continue to be major participants in the process and to build on current reforms to policing. However, in the longer term, it may be thought that the need for restorative practice to be seen as independent, impartial and easily identifiable to the public may dictate the institution of a national body with a specific restorative justice brief (such as the ATA in Austria). This would ensure the independent organisation and facilitation of mediation and conferencing; the overseeing of national standards and training; the keeping of statistics and the dissemination of information. It would also give restorative justice an identity and this would help to promote its philosophy, as well as to encourage a continuing dialogue between theory and practice.

Other involvement in restorative justice

There is a range of other initiatives provided by both voluntary and statutory sectors. Both NACRO and SOVA provide services for statutory agencies with which they are in partnership and Mediation UK provides training and accreditation for its affiliated mediation services. For example, West Kent Independent Mediation Service operates with a team of trained volunteer mediators, working under a paid coordinator. They offer victim-offender mediation, as well as the community service. REMEDI, in South Yorkshire, is another victim-offender mediation service and is now one of the Home Office funded crime reduction partnership projects. AMENDS also operates with volunteer mediators, offering neighbour and victim-offender mediation, as well as restorative justice conferencing. Victim empathy and awareness, and weapons and drug awareness programmes are also available.

The West Midlands Victim Offender Unit was established in 1985 and is now wholly funded by the probation service. It is staffed by paid employees and, although originally offender-focused, has a reputation for neutrality, dealing with both adult and youth cases. Referrals come from the courts, defence solicitors or the probation service. However, most interventions are pre-sentence and participation will be taken into account by the courts. The unit is well-recognised and most participants have been satisfied with the process: 80 per cent reported that they would recommend it to others.[6] This is by no means an exhaustive list of what is on offer but it illustrates that provision is patchy and ad hoc. It points to the desirability of an integrated system and national standards of training and practice, to increase availability and to safeguard standards.

There is a strong interest in restorative practice in prison, spearheaded by Tim Newell, former governor of a therapeutic prison (Grendon Underwood) and others and supported by many staff. There are a variety of schemes already running:

- Bristol prison has appointed the first prison restorative justice coordinator: they are planning to explore balancing the concerns of victims and communities with the resettlement of offenders should be;
- Huntercombe HMYOI is experimenting with adjourning governors' adjudications for conferences; incorporating contracts with victims at the beginning and end of sentences; and using conferencing to settle disputes before they escalate;
- Hull and The Mount prisons are developing victim empathy;

- HMYOI Aylesbury offers victim-offender conferencing;
- HMYOI Lancaster Farms is running projects with inmates undertaking restorative work in the local community;
- HMP Holme House has inmates maintaining and restoring local parks;
- HMP Bullingdon is building a restorative element into punishment, involving victim-offender work; and
- HMYOI Brinsford runs a victim-offender mediation programme in partnership with Sandwell mediation service. Meetings include building in support, which will continue after release to assist in resettlement. This is an example of 'circling' similar to that in operation in Minnesota.

We were given an example of a case involving a 14-year-old boy serving six months for arson, who was referred to the mediation service on remand and continued the contact throughout his sentence. The offence had created damage costing about £80,000 and this boy, one of several involved, had, in his words, 'only lit the paper'. The victim wanted him to understand the impact on her and her family and to accept his part in it. She had had to move home, had lost nearly all of her possessions, including all family photos, videos and personal items. Her two young daughters had suffered nightmares and panic attacks about what would have happened if the family had been in the house. One daughter was frightened of showers, as they brought on memories of water dripping throughout the house as the fire brigade attempted to douse the flames. The other daughter was upset by the death of her goldfish – to which she attributed symbolic significance. Hearing about these human traumas had its effect, making the boy understand that without his participation, the incident would never have occurred. He could identify most with the children and wrote a letter centred on this. He also managed to save enough money to buy the children a new fish tank and two goldfish, delivered to the family by the mediator. The victim remained angry but also found some room for compassion for him, knowing that he had lost his liberty, and this made a meeting possible just before the boy's release. They were each able to build on the work already done and express their feelings in a manageable way, so that they left feeling much more able to get on with their lives.

Crime Reduction Partnership Projects are relatively new projects – still in their early stages – funded by the Home Office in a variety of different settings. They demonstrate the government's support for restorative justice and its interest in obtaining evidence about effectiveness. Unfortunately, it has been difficult to obtain much information about progress and we have only been able to talk informally to people running them. Results will not be known until 2007. The schemes are being run by the Justice Research Consortium, a partnership of criminal justice and research agencies, drawing upon the international experience of Heather Strang from Canberra (the RISE project) and Larry Sherman from the University of Philadelphia.

Magistrates' court cases in Northumbria and Crown Court cases in London are being diverted, with the intention of testing whether crime reduces. The research design entails randomised control sampling, so that rates of recidivism among people who have had conferences can be compared with those of a group who have not. While judges are not bound by any agreement reached, they may take into account any additional information received as a result when considering sentence.

The London study involves adults appearing in five Crown Courts who are invited to take part in conferences after conviction. At the time of writing, about 85 per cent of offenders have wanted to participate and about 60 per cent of victims have actually attended meetings before sentence. The Inspector (Brian Dowling) who manages the London scheme, has so far found that victims like to make arrangements speedily, although this is somewhat at odds with the experience of Youth Offending Teams, who have found that victims need time. He attributes the relatively high level of victim participation to the reassuring nature of police presence for victims, both psychologically and in terms of safety. No figures or findings are available at this early stage, which is frustrating, as clearly the opportunities for learning are great.

As with other police-run conferences, the facilitators have been trained to apply a problem-solving approach, using scripted questions and techniques, although intervention is supposed to be kept to a minimum. We have heard that participants' perspectives about the real nature of the problem, and thus the solution, often change. Inspector Dowling comments that while some victims remain critical of what they regard as lenient sentences, others feel differently once they know more about the defendant's background and circumstances. Some have left conferences feeling much better and more reassured than when they went in.

The magistrates' courts project is running along the same lines and it has been similarly difficult to gather any reliable information about it yet. Research and results for both schemes will not be known until 2007.

At the other end of the process, a study of post-sentence conferences within the community will look at the effects of conferences on those who receive community rehabilitation or community rehabilitation and punishment orders. Participants are assessed for suitability (drug and alcohol problems will preclude attendance) before sentence and interviewed again before the conference. It is said in relation to these that victims often need time to consider participation. Conferences are now being offered in prisons, to those convicted of robbery, street crime, serious assaults and burglaries. Sex-offenders may not participate but, of the others, 70 per cent agreed to take part and victims have not been as unwilling to attend as feared. Agreements may include undertakings to participate in programmes, such as drug rehabilitation or anger management, and it is to be hoped that such opportunities are realistically available in our very overcrowded prisons. Apologies are usually forthcoming and agreements are monitored at three-, six- and 12-month stages. Feedback has so far been positive.

The Connect Restorative Justice Project is a two-year Home Office pilot project, established in 2001, to examine restorative practice with adults. It is managed by NACRO, in partnership with the probation service and is available to defendants at Camberwell Green and Tower Bridge Magistrates' Courts. It was originally intended to be restricted to cases not attracting custody but more serious cases have been included as the project has developed.

Connect was expected to receive referrals purely from the probation service but magistrates and district judges have increasingly asked project staff to be present at court in order to make direct referrals themselves. The team examines requests for pre-sentence reports, in order to pick out cases with an identifiable victim where mediation could be of value. They have become more interested in the relationship between the parties, rather than the apparent seriousness of the offence: a Nils Christie approach. The human factors are often complex and three-week adjournments do not usually allow sufficient time to arrange conferences. However, it may be sufficient for direct or indirect mediation and, certainly, effort goes into making a restorative intervention of some kind.

Connect's manager believes that the existing system often propels victims into the process too early, so that they end up serving the needs of the system. His impression is that for many victims the point of recovery is the best time and, in order to serve their interests, Connect's work has extended to allow for this. He quoted the example of someone seriously injured in a car accident being given a year's notice of the offender's release. By the time it arrived, the injured man felt that he would like to communicate his suffering, so as to try to avoid any repetition. It proved to be the right time and was beneficial for both parties.

Connect believes that it has developed an effective victim perspective: victims have on the whole been appreciative of the opportunity to express themselves and the project is finding that, although this is resource intensive, it is vital for success. Courts have welcomed Connect's reports and have generally acted upon them. We were given an example of a neighbourhood dispute where the victim was adamant that he wanted nothing further to do with the offender and did not want compensation. Connect were able to communicate this to the district judge, who respected his wishes.

The staff would like to diversify and offer a generic service, providing a range of options, to which people could have direct access. They wish to provide a service in more cases of domestic violence, for instance, as they believe it is more likely to be successful than alternative action (or inaction). This would require extra training but the manager is convinced that the service should be available and that, therefore, there needs to be an expansion to allow for appropriate interventions in more serious offences.

Towards answers

Restorative justice is, therefore, flourishing in a variety of diverse settings both in our own and other countries. We next consider the principles and conclusions, which have emerged from all the activities reported.

Notes

1 J Braithwaite, *Crime, Shame and Reintegration* (Cambridge University Press, 1989).
2 C Hoyle, R Young and R Hill, *Proceed with Caution* (Joseph Rowntree Foundation, York Publishing Services, 2002).
3 Including Declan Roche, *Accountability in Restorative Justice* (Oxford University Press, 2003).
4 Young, 2001.
5 See RISE statistics.
6 D Miers et al, *An Exploratory Evaluation of Restorative Justice Schemes* (Crime Reduction Research Series Paper 9, Research, Development and Statistics Directorate, 2001).

Chapter 10 – Conclusions and the way forward

Restorative justice is still at an early stage in its development. Our understanding of it is expanding and evolving in line with policy and practice – both at home and abroad – described in preceding chapters. We know we have much to learn and this is what makes restorative justice such a challenging and exciting concept. Here and now, it is becoming a feature of the criminal justice system; and the proactive spirit of the government's strategy document supports the advances made by individuals, projects and policymakers in many parts of the world. Indeed, it may put us ahead of a considerable number of other countries, depending on implementation and public response.

Restorative justice started on a wave of euphoria, when early experiments revealed how much victims (who had long been excluded) could benefit from being able to express their views and feelings within a controlled and constructive setting. Being properly heard is a powerful experience and it enabled victims to shed the burden of their anxieties. Being able to hear, to explain the background to their actions and to try to put things right was found to be equally meaningful for offenders. This seemed the ideal: the squaring of the circle: of benefit both to the individuals concerned and to wider society. That initial enthusiasm is not diminished and those we met in the course of our research continue to express it. However, they, and we collectively, are now much more aware that restorative justice is not a panacea. It has disadvantages as well as advantages and unless properly and appropriately used will not deliver its potential benefits: the relief of victims' fears, consideration of the causes of offending, the reintegration of both parties and the safety of society. We have reviewed these factors, taking note of the demands by academics and practitioners to be realistic about restorative justice and not to risk raising public expectations to such a degree that perceived failure of its methods results in them being discarded.

Human rights standards are integral to the legal framework and we have pointed to the creative role played by international conventions in the spreading of restorative practice for young people. However, the question of legal representation, and the contribution of lawyers generally, is a central part of the current debate. The courts have intervened to require such representation where young people have not, or may not, be able to participate effectively in informal processes or where they have not been given sufficient legal advice. There is a fine line between direct communication with offenders and dominating them. Where young people are emotionally, intellectually or psychologically disadvantaged (and these difficulties cannot otherwise be overcome), youth offender panels may need to grant representation.

Human rights principles are closely intertwined with the question of accountability and here work is proceeding – nationally and internationally – to achieve practice standards that will ensure impartiality and independence, without being so prescriptive that the flexible, problem-solving nature of restorative justice is compromised. We have outlined (in chapter 3) more detailed arguments about tactics that might assist, and there are UN and Council of Europe directives and recommendations on the same subject.

The lessons from our research show us that more research is needed, especially in relation to victims and the effects of the new practice on them. What we do not need more research about is the current system and the ineffectiveness of prison. There is a growing consensus that our overcrowded prisons have little rehabilitative potential; and that the constant raising of penalties has done nothing to alleviate the dissatisfaction of victims, the high rates of recidivism, and the continuing fears of society. Many argue that some of the provisions in the Criminal Justice Act 2003, such as the disproportionate penalising of persistent offenders (the very people with whom we most need to be working on the causes of their behaviour) and the lengthening of other sentences will not protect society in the longer term. This is because the majority are still serving short sentences, expressly admitted by the Chief Inspector of Prisons and others to be disruptive and having little offer to anyone.

Overwhelmingly, we are incarcerating those from emotionally deprived backgrounds, with serious educational and mental health problems, who have often been homeless and usually unemployed before going to prison. Suicide and self-harm in custody is rising, despite increased awareness and training; and there is no sense of a viable future for people with such disadvantages. We acknowledge recent efforts to improve resettlement, but much more needs to be done.

These policies have been failing society badly; and it is the recognition of this failure that has led to the current interest in alternative methods, and hence helped to make space for restorative practice. We have taken an inventory of the difficulties: and the question now is how to change a landscape which will otherwise feature more prisons, fewer answers for victims, less rehabilitation for offenders, and - because there is no real resolution of the fundamentals - an even more fearful society. This is a taxing proposition and a difficult area of policy. We need to come to terms with the fact that prison remains attractive to the public and the press in the short-term, although its negative consequences are now well-documented and it is known to be counter-productive in the longer term.

It is this self-imposed downward spiral that has created – encouragingly – an opportunity for restorative practice. It is imperative, if this picture is not to deteriorate further, that credible and effective alternatives are supplied. Until we have them, it is unlikely that attitudes will shift towards a more realistic direction. One of the objectives of restorative justice, by looking at causes, is to link criminal justice with social justice, in a quest for more constructive solutions.

At the same time, our research demonstrates that restorative practice itself needs to be tried and tested; it does not have all the answers. We have seen that it will not always be suitable: victims must not be pressurised to participate, some offenders will not be remorseful and others will be too damaged to be able to empathise. Agreements will not always be kept and it is unlikely that there will be sufficient resources to respond adequately to all the difficulties uncovered by restorative processes. This means that there should be a continuing dialogue between theory and practice, so that learning continues. We believe that there should be a national body to facilitate these and other requirements discussed in this report and to establish an identity and philosophy, which are necessary for public understanding and coherent development.

Such conclusions as we have been able to draw from impressionistic research in a rapidly changing field indicate that, if restorative practice in this country is to advance, and to be effective, it should be seen as:

1. **A set of values that informs a range of specific practices rather than one particular model of provision**
    Central to the criminal justice system is the need for change – of the offender's conduct and the victim's experience. The government's strategy response, perhaps understandably, focuses on programmes with defined objectives and detailed action plans. The danger is that restorative justice is 'mainstreamed' mechanistically: it is a philosophy for dealing more sensitively and effectively with human beings and must not be debased into rituals. It is about a frame of mind that should infuse the whole criminal justice system.

2.   **A framework within which the criminal justice system can move away from over-reliance on punitive imprisonment**
The government itself has acknowledged that:

> *Too often, short-sentence prisoners leave custody just as illiterate, as unemployable and as prone to drug dependence as when they went in.*[1]

And:

> *Custody has an important role to play in punishing offenders and protecting the public. But it is an expensive resource which should be focused on dangerous, serious, seriously persistent offenders … It is imperative that we have a correctional system which punishes but also reduces reoffending through the rehabilitation of the offender and his or her reintegration into the community.*[2]

Restorative justice offers both a way of diverting offenders to more constructive options, both before and after trial and sentence, as well as working positively with them while in prison and after release.

3.   **Realistic and responsive**
Diversity and flexibility are critical in dealing with individual circumstances. There is no definitive model and 'one size' is never likely to fit all. It can and should be used across the spectrum of offending in a variety of different ways but it must be used appropriately, respecting victims' wishes and offenders' attitudes and capabilities.

The most controversial and difficult area in which to develop restorative justice is in the more serious cases: those that fall above the level where diversion would be generally accepted and below the level where restorative justice was simply being applied to inform sentence planning. This will test the extent to which it can be an alternative not an addition and could be a good use of the new community sentences enacted in the Criminal Justice Act 2003.

4.   **Adequately resourced both in terms of amount per case and in terms of the length of time for which funding is provided to restorative justice projects**
The precariousness of funding for restorative justice projects has seriously damaged attempts to evaluate their work in the past.   The threat to

continuity has had an undermining effect on what is, essentially, a scheme requiring time and resources to establish and implement. As we have seen, it can only operate as intended if attitudes and values shift. Equally, outcomes of restorative events must be funded in order for them to have any meaning, or longer term impact.

5. **Designed to avoid 'net -widening'**
Net-widening is the process by which offenders are swept into sentencing, cautioning or diversionary programmes when, otherwise, they might have been dealt with more informally and diverted out of the criminal justice system to better effect. We are concerned, in particular, that restorative cautioning schemes might act in such a way and that, apart from the misuse of resources, rehabilitation may be jeopardised by the police record that results, potentially affecting future prospects.

6. **Consistent with the principles of human rights**
The requirements for fair trial and due process must be respected, including access to legal representation where necessary. Sentencing must be proportionate. The structure of referral orders has, so far, avoided legal challenge but those developing restorative justice within the criminal justice system will need to ensure impartiality, independence, and proper safeguards.

7. **Supported by the development of standards for practice and the accountability of practitioners**
We note that the drive for standards and accountability internationally has come through bodies such as the United Nations and represent attempts to integrate human rights principles within restorative justice practice. We agree that the government is right in its strategy paper 'to consult carefully about how to develop effective practice, training and accreditation'.[3]

8. **Conducted by independent practitioners**
We raise the issue of the extent to, and the way in which, police and prosecution participation is appropriate in restorative justice programmes. In the longer term, we consider that the police should withdraw from the conduct of restorative cautioning though remain fully involved in the decision to divert to cautioning and that they should instead be involved in the process as contributing participants.

9. **Led by a single body to oversee its development**

This should not be a large bureaucracy and discussions are needed as to its establishment and remit. However, it should be headed by representatives of the major stakeholders in the criminal justice system and be representative of the demographics of the country, with a small supporting staff whose role will be: to promote the philosophy underlying restorative justice; to provide an identity; to formulate standards; to monitor; and to facilitate dialogue between theory and practice. The Youth Justice Board is a useful model in some respects, although much too large for these purposes.

10. **Championed by government**

Ministers need to reconcile acceptance of restorative justice principles with the rhetoric of being tough on crime. They need to drive public opinion rather than follow it and to put the emphasis on the way in which the criminal justice system needs to be targeted towards changing the behaviour of individual offenders and the experience of individual victims. We need the Home Secretary to maintain and expand upon his enthusiasm as expressed in the foreword to the government's restorative justice strategy:

> *Restorative conferencing, when victims, offenders, their supporters and other citizens come together to deal with the aftermath of crime, is an example of active communities at their best – local people coming together, facilitated by the State, to solve local problems ... I believe that restorative justice can have an important part to play at all stages of the criminal justice system ...*

The way forward

Incorporation into the criminal justice system is itself a huge undertaking and one that will demand continuing commitment over a long period. However, even in the face of such an enterprise, it is important to look beyond to new horizons and possibilities. The government strategy paper does this, by asking whether restorative justice should be used for sensitive cases such as domestic violence, race hate and homophobia. Many of the responses to the consultation paper did not favour the use of restorative practice in domestic violence cases. We beg to differ.

Experience in Austria has shown that although the women's movement originally objected to victim-offender mediation in such a context, they have now changed their minds. They found that, although recidivism rates might not be significantly different, the process was helpful for women. It provided a controlled environment in which they could articulate and express the problems and this boosted their self-confidence, making it easier for them to recognise and assess their options. Cases are, of course, screened particularly carefully, because many will not be suitable but, even so, these findings are encouraging.

They suggested that a well-considered pilot project – perhaps using similarly specialised techniques and training – would be an innovation that may give us further ideas about what has long been regarded as one of the more intractable social problems. Domestic violence represents a high proportion of crime and it features in the background of many women offenders.

We found no specific information on other sensitive cases in the course of our research. However, it is logical that a similar approach may be applicable to race hate and homophobia, as they also require responses with an educational element. Indeed, restorative justice and related approaches have a potential role in responding to very many kinds of conflicts from an international level downwards. Domestically, restorative practice in criminal justice forms part of a broader approach to dealing with troublesome and difficult behaviour in local neighbourhoods, schools and workplaces, as well as specifically criminal activity. It is an approach that places a premium on taking responsibility for offending, for putting things right and on making arrangements for a less problematic future.

Notes

1 *Criminal Justice: the way ahead* (CM 5074, 2001), p13.
2 *Justice for All* (CM 5563, 2002), para 5.6.
3 *Restorative Justice: the government's strategy*, 2003, p37.

Appendix 1 – Extracts from Conventions

European Convention on Human Rights
Article 5 – Right to liberty and security

1. Everyone has the right to liberty and security of person. No one shall be deprived of his liberty save in the following cases and in accordance with a procedure prescribed by law:

    a) the lawful detention of a person after conviction by a competent court;

    b) the lawful arrest or detention of a person for non-compliance with the lawful order of a court or in order to secure the fulfilment of any obligation prescribed by law;

    c) the lawful arrest or detention of a person effected for the purpose of bringing him before the competent legal authority on reasonable suspicion of having committed an offence or when it is reasonably considered necessary to prevent his committing an offence or fleeing after having done so;

    d) the detention of a minor by lawful order for the purpose of educational supervision or his lawful detention for the purpose of bringing him before the competent legal authority;

    e) the lawful detention of persons for the prevention of spreading infectious diseases, of persons of unsound mind, alcoholics or drug addicts or vagrants;

    f) the lawful arrest or detention of a person to prevent his effecting an unauthorised entry into the country or of a person against whom action is being taken with a view to deportation or extradition.

2. Everyone who is arrested shall be informed promptly, in a language which he understands, of the reasons for his arrest and any charge against him.

3. Everyone arrested or detained in accordance with the provisions of paragraph 1.c of this article shall be brought promptly before a judge or other officer authorised by law to exercise judicial power and shall be entitled to trial within a reasonable time or to release pending trial. Release may be conditioned by guarantees to appear for trial.

4. Everyone who is deprived of his liberty by arrest or detention shall be entitled to take proceedings by which the lawfulness of his detention shall

be decided speedily by a court and his release ordered if the detention is not lawful.

5.   Everyone who has been the victim of arrest or detention in contravention of the provisions of this article shall have an enforceable right to compensation.

Article 6 – Right to a fair trial

1.   In the determination of his civil rights and obligations or of any criminal charge against him, everyone is entitled to a fair and public hearing within a reasonable time by an independent and impartial tribunal established by law. Judgment shall be pronounced publicly but the press and public may be excluded from all or part of the trial in the interests of morals, public order or national security in a democratic society, where the interests of juveniles or the protection of the private life of the parties so require, or to the extent strictly necessary in the opinion of the court in special circumstances where publicity would prejudice the interests of justice.

2.   Everyone charged with a criminal offence shall be presumed innocent until proved guilty according to law.

3.   Everyone charged with a criminal offence has the following minimum rights:
     a)   to be informed, promptly, in a language in which he understands and in detail, of the nature and cause of the accusation against him;
     b)   to have adequate time and facilities for the preparation of his defence;
     c)   to defend himself in person or through legal assistance of his own choosing or, if he has not sufficient means to pay for legal assistance, to be given it free when the interests of justice so require;
     d)   to examine, or have examined witnesses against him and to obtain the attendance and examination of witnesses on his behalf under the same conditions as witnesses against him;
     e)   to have the free assistance of an interpreter if he cannot understand or speak the language used in court.

Article 8 – Right to respect for private and family life

1.   Everyone has the right to respect for his private and family life, his home and his correspondence.

2.   There shall be no interference by a public authority with the exercise of this

right except such as is in accordance with the law and is necessary in a democratic society in the interests of national security, public safety or the economic well-being of the country, for the prevention of disorder or crime, for the protection of health or morals, or for the protection of the rights and freedoms of others.

United Nations International Convention on the Rights of the Child 1989

Article 12.1

States Parties shall assure to the child who is capable of forming his or her own views the right to express those views freely in all matters affecting the child, the views of the child being given due weight in accordance with the age and maturity of the child.

Article 12.2

For this purpose, the child shall in particular be provided the opportunity to be heard in any judicial and administrative proceedings affecting the child, either directly, or through a representative or an appropriate body, in a manner consistent with the procedural rules of national law.

Article 13.1

The child shall have the right to freedom of expression; this right shall include freedom to seek, receive and impart information and ideas of all kinds, regardless of frontiers, either orally, in writing or in print, in the form of art, or through any other media of the child's choice.

Article 13.2

The exercise of this right may be subject to certain restrictions, but these shall only be such as are provided by law and are necessary:
a) for respect of the rights or reputations of others; or
b) for the protection of national security or of public order, or of public health or morals.

Article 15.1

States Parties recognize the rights of the child to freedom of association and to freedom of peaceful assembly.

Article 15.2

No restrictions may be placed on the exercise of these rights other than those imposed in conformity with the law and which are necessary in a democratic society in the interests of national security or public safety, public order, the protection of public health or morals or the protection of the rights and freedoms of others.

Article 16.1
No child shall be subjected to arbitrary or unlawful interference with his or her privacy, family, home or correspondence, nor to unlawful attacks on his or her honour and reputation.

Article 16.2
The child has the right to the protection of the law against such interference or attacks.

Article 37(b)
No child shall be deprived of his or her liberty unlawfully or arbitrarily. The arrest, detention or imprisonment of a child shall be in conformity with the law and shall be used only as a measure of last resort and for the shortest appropriate period of time.

Article 37(d)
Every child deprived of his or her liberty shall have the right to prompt access to legal and other appropriate assistance, as well as the right to challenge the legality of the deprivation of his or her liberty before a court or other competent, independent and impartial authority, and to a prompt decision on any such action.

Article 40.1
States Parties recognize the right of every child alleged as, accused of, or recognized as having infringed the penal law to be treated in a manner consistent with the promotion of the child's sense of dignity and worth, which reinforces the child's respect for the human rights and fundamental freedoms of others and which takes into account the child's age and the desirability of promoting the child's reintegration and the child's assuming a constructive role in society.

Article 40.2(b)
Every child alleged as or accused of having infringed the penal law has at least the following guarantees:
   i)   to be presumed innocent until proven guilty according to law;
   ii) to be informed promptly and directly of the charges against him or her,

and, if appropriate, through his or her parents or legal guardians, and to have legal or other appropriate assistance in the preparation and presentation of his or her defence;

iii) to have the matter determined without delay by a competent, independent and impartial authority or judicial body in a fair hearing according to law, in the presence of legal or other appropriate assistance and, unless it is considered not to be in the best interest of the child, in particular, taking into account his or her age or situation, his or her parents or legal guardians;

iv) not to be compelled to give testimony or to confess guilt; to examine or have examined adverse witnesses and to obtain the participation and examination of witnesses on his or her behalf under conditions of equality;

v) if considered to have infringed the penal law, to have this decision and any measures imposed in consequence thereof reviewed by a higher competent, independent and impartial authority or judicial body according to law;

vi) to have the free assistance of an interpreter if the child cannot understand or speak the language used;

vii) to have his or her privacy fully respected at all stages of the proceedings.

Article 40.3

States Parties shall seek to promote the establishment of laws, procedures, authorities and institutions specifically applicable to children alleged as, accused of, or recognized as having infringed the penal law and in particular:

a) the establishment of a minimum age below which children shall be presumed not to have the capacity to infringe the penal law;

b) whenever appropriate and desirable, measures for dealing with such children without resorting to judicial proceedings, providing that human rights and legal safeguards are fully respected.

Article 40.4

A variety of dispositions, such as care, guidance and supervision orders; counselling; probation; foster care; education and vocational training programmes and other alternatives to institutional care shall be available to ensure that children are dealt with in a manner appropriate to their well-being and proportionate both to their circumstances and the offence.

International Covenant on Civil and Political Rights 1966
Article 10(2)(b)
Accused juvenile persons shall be separated from adults and brought as speedily as possible for adjudication.

Article 14(4)
In the case of juvenile persons the procedure shall be such as will take account of their age and desirability of promoting their rehabilitation.

United Nations Rules for the Protection of Juveniles Deprived of their Liberty 1990
Rule 1
The juvenile justice system should uphold the rights and safety and promote the physical and mental well-being of juveniles. Imprisonment should be used as a last resort.

Rule 3
The Rules are intended to establish minimum standards accepted by the United Nations for the protection of juveniles deprived of their liberty in all forms, consistent with human rights and fundamental freedoms, and with a view to counteracting the detrimental effects of all types of detention and to fostering integration in society.

Rule 13
Juveniles deprived of their liberty shall not for any reason related to their status be denied the civil, economic, political, social or cultural rights to which they are entitled under national or international law, and which are compatible with the deprivation of liberty.

United Nations Guidelines for the Prevention of Juvenile Delinquency 1990 (the 'Riyadh Guidelines')
Fundamental principles
1. The prevention of juvenile delinquency is an essential part of crime prevention in society. By engaging in lawful, socially useful activities and adopting a humanistic orientation towards society and outlook on life, young persons can develop non-criminogenic attitudes.

2. The successful prevention of juvenile delinquency requires efforts on the part of the entire society to ensure the harmonious development of adolescents, with respect for and promotion of their personality from early childhood.

3. For the purposes of the interpretation of the present guidelines, a child-centred orientation should be pursued. Young persons should have an active role and partnership within society and should not be considered as mere objects of socialisation or control.

4. In the implementation of the present guidelines, in accordance with national legal systems, the well-being of young persons from their early childhood should be the focus of any preventive programme.

5. The need for and importance of progressive delinquency prevention policies and the systematic study and the elaboration of measures should be recognised. These should avoid criminalising and penalising a child for behaviour that does not cause serious damage to the development of the child or harm to others. Such policies and measures should involve:

a) the provision of opportunities, in particular educational opportunities, to meet the varying needs of young persons and to serve as a supportive framework for safeguarding the personal development of all young persons, particularly those who are demonstrably endangered or at social risk and are in need of special care and protection;
b) specialised philosophies and approaches for delinquency prevention, on the basis of laws, processes, institutions, facilities and a service delivery network aimed at reducing the motivation, need and opportunity for, or conditions giving rise to, the commission of infractions;
c) official intervention to be pursued primarily in the overall interest of the young person and guided by fairness and equity;
d) safeguarding the well-being, development, rights and interests of all young persons;
e) consideration that youthful behaviour or conduct that does not conform to overall social norms and values is often part of the maturation and growth process and tends to disappear spontaneously in most individuals with the transition to adulthood;
f) awareness that, in the predominant opinion of experts, labelling a young person as 'deviant', 'delinquent' or 'pre-delinquent' often contributes to the development of a consistent pattern of undesirable behaviour by young persons.

6. Community-based services and programmes should be developed for the prevention of juvenile delinquency, particularly where no agencies have yet

been established. Formal agencies of social control should only be utilised as a means of last resort.

46. The institutionalisation of young persons should be a measure of last resort and for the minimum necessary period, and the best interests of the young person should be of paramount importance.

United Nations Standard Minimum Rules for the Administration of Juvenile Justice 1985 (the 'Beijing Rules')
Rule 1.4

Juvenile justice shall be conceived as an integral part of the national development process of each country, within a comprehensive framework of social justice for all juveniles, thus, at the same time, contributing to the protection of the young and the maintenance of a peaceful order in society.

Rule 1.6

Juvenile justice services shall be systematically developed and coordinated with a view to improving and sustaining the competence of personnel involved in the services, including their methods, approaches and attitudes.

Rule 5.1

The juvenile justice system shall emphasise the well-being of the juvenile and shall ensure that any reaction to juvenile offenders shall always be in proportion to the circumstances of both the offenders and the offence.

Rule 6.1

In view of the varying special needs of juveniles as well as the variety of measures available, appropriate scope for discretion shall be allowed at all stages of proceedings and at the different levels of juvenile justice administration, including investigation, prosecution, adjudication and the follow-up of dispositions.

Rule 7.1

Basic procedural safeguards such as the presumption of innocence, the right to be notified of the charges, the right to remain silent, the right to counsel, the right to the presence of a parent or guardian, the right to confront and cross-examine witnesses and the right to appeal to a higher authority shall be guaranteed at all stages of proceedings.

Rule 8.1

The juvenile's right to privacy shall be respected at all stages in order to avoid harm being caused to her or him by undue publicity or by the process of labelling.

Rule 8.2

In principle, no information that may lead to the identification of a juvenile offender shall be published.

Rule 11.1

Consideration shall be given, wherever appropriate, to dealing with juvenile offenders without resorting to formal trial by the competent authority, referred to in rule 14.1 below.

Rule 11.2

The police, the prosecution or other agencies dealing with juvenile cases shall be empowered to dispose of such cases, at their discretion, without recourse to formal hearings, in accordance with the criteria laid down for that purpose in the respective legal system and also in accordance with the principles contained in these Rules.

Rule 11.3

Any diversion involving referral to appropriate community or other services shall require the consent of the juvenile, or her or his parents or guardian, provided that such decision to refer a case shall be subject to review by a competent authority, upon application.

Rule 11.4

In order to facilitate the discretionary disposition of juvenile cases, efforts shall be made to provide for community programmes, such as temporary supervision and guidance, restitution, and compensation of victims.

Rule 12.1

In order to best fulfil their functions, police officers who frequently or exclusively deal with juveniles or who are primarily engaged in the prevention of juvenile crime shall be specially instructed and trained. In large cities, special police units should be established for that purpose.

Rule 13.1
Detention pending trial shall be used only as a measure of last resort and for the shortest possible period of time.

Rule 13.2
Whenever possible, detention pending trial shall be replaced by alternative measures, such as close supervision, intensive care or placement with a family or in an educational setting or home.

Rule 13.3
Juveniles under detention pending trial shall be entitled to all rights and guarantees of the Standard Minimum Rules for the Treatment of Prisoners adopted by the United Nations.

Rule 13.4
Juveniles under detention pending trial shall be kept separate from adults and shall be detained in a separate institution or in a separate part of an institution also holding adults.

Rule 13.5
While in custody, juveniles shall receive care, protection and all necessary individual assistance – social, educational, vocational, psychological, medical and physical – that they may require in view of their age, sex and personality.

Rule 18.1
A large variety of disposition measures shall be made available to the competent authority, allowing for flexibility so as to avoid institutionalisation to the greatest extent possible. Such measures, some of which may be combined, include:

a) care, guidance and supervision orders;
b) probation;
c) community service orders;
d) financial penalties, compensation and restitution;
e) intermediate treatment and other treatment orders;
f) orders to participate in group counselling and similar activities;
g) orders concerning foster care, living communities or other educational settings;
h) other relevant orders.

Rule 19.1
The placement of a juvenile in an institution shall always be a disposition of last resort and for the minimum necessary period.

Rule 20.1
Each case shall from the outset be handled expeditiously, without any unnecessary delay.

Rule 21.1
Records of juvenile offenders shall be kept strictly confidential and closed to third parties. Access to such records shall be limited to persons directly concerned with the disposition of the case at hand or other duly authorised persons.

Rule 21.2
Records of juvenile offenders shall not be used in adult proceedings in subsequent cases involving the same offender.

Rule 30.1
Efforts shall be made to organise and promote necessary research as a basis for effective planning and policy formulation.

Rule 30.2
Efforts shall be made to review and appraise periodically the trends, problems and causes of juvenile delinquency and crime as well as the varying particular needs of juveniles in custody.

Rule 30.3
Efforts shall be made to establish a regular evaluative research mechanism built into the system of juvenile justice administration and to collect and analyse relevant data and information for appropriate assessment and future improvement and reform of the administration.

Rule 30.4
The delivery of services in juvenile justice administration shall be systematically planned and implemented as an integral part of national development efforts.

Appendix 2 – Responses to the government's strategy paper

The government strategy paper asked a number of specific questions about restorative justice. Below, we repeat certain ones on which we feel we can make a contribution.

Q1:   *What should be the main principles for the use of restorative justice in a criminal justice context? Should these differ from principles for restorative justice outside the criminal justice system?*

Q2:   *What would be the benefits and disadvantages of developing more specific principles in particular areas – for example for sensitive offences such as hate crimes, sex crimes and domestic violence?*

JUSTICE has only considered the criminal justice context in this report but the thrust of our argument, ie, that restorative practice puts criminal justice firmly within a wider social justice context, suggests that although different techniques may be helpful, the principles are of wide application.

However, our research has thrown up different attitudes towards sensitive offences. In Austria, where there is an independent, professional cadre of mediators who have special training and use refined techniques, domestic violence mediation seems to have become popular and successful. Women's reservations appear to have been largely dispelled as experience demonstrated that mediation did not demote the gravity of the offending; and helped women to articulate their fears and feelings, thus gaining more control over their situations. In Norway, on the other hand, racially-motivated, sex-offending and domestic violence are likely not to be diverted to mediation because they are regarded as too serious or intractable. Mediators in Norway are volunteers and we report concerns about the quality of their training and, therefore, preparation: essential ingredients, as death row work in Texas also shows, for more serious or emotionally charged cases.

This suggests that it is practice, rather than principles, which merit particular attention. In Austria, there are two mediators instead of one allocated to domestic violence cases in order to deal with the likely imbalance of power. In Texas, training for mediators undertaking sensitive death row cases is especially intensive and preparation is expected to take much longer.

*Q4:   Do you will agree that there is the need for a range of training providers, with a
       shared approach to training and accreditation for restorative justice
       practitioners? If so, what might this look like?*

*Q24:   The value of community involvement through the use of volunteers needs to be
       balanced with making use of the expertise of criminal justice professionals.
       What combination of criminal justice professionals, other professionals and
       volunteers should deliver restorative justice?*

While we did not inquire into the nuts and bolts of training and accreditation
arrangements, our research shows the importance of these in relation to
accountability and standards. We felt that there were more advantages in having
an independent body of practitioners – professional or voluntary – whose core
business is restorative justice. There should be representation from all the
different interest groups but bureaucracy should be kept to a minimum and the
secretariat does not need to be large. Although such a body will need to monitor
standards and training; keep statistics; provide information and give restorative
justice a profile and an identity; it will not have the wider range of functions and
responsibilities of, for example, the Youth Justice Board. Such a body would be
much more likely to maintain the philosophy underlying restorative justice,
which is essential to its proper practice.

The police – Thames Valley Police in particular – have made a substantial
contribution to the development of restorative justice. However, they are not, in
the longer term, the correct place to site restorative justice interventions. This is
not to undervalue their work and they have a crucial role to play both as
participants in conferences and as gatekeepers. However, their performance of
other police functions means, inevitably, that they cannot satisfy the
requirement that they be perceived as fair. It is a confusion of roles. Although
there may be advantages in the reassurance police have to offer victims,
offenders are unlikely to be able to see them as fair, no matter how well-trained
or how skilful as facilitators they may be. Equally, police stations should not be
used as venues for conferences, for the same reasons.

Q14:   What are the best ways to raise awareness of reparation by offenders?

*Q19:   How, and with whom, should the government work to increase understanding of
       restorative justice a) among criminal justice and other professionals and b) the
       wider public?*

If we had such a recognised national body, awareness and understanding would automatically rise. Such a group – operating with professional standards and clear goals – would be able to lobby government and acquire an input into decision-making. Their perspective would be greatly in demand, as the Restorative Justice Consortium has demonstrated.

However, the government should also take the initiative with the media, who have helped to sustain the punitive attitudes that have ignored both the causes of offending and the long-term interests of victims. One leading national newspaper has already run a number of positive articles in recent months and sponsored relevant events. This is a strategy that helped to mobilise public support in Austria, where there was a similar problem of having too many young people incarcerated.

Q18:   What other possible future developments in criminal justice could be combined with restorative approaches?

There is growing interest in circles in this country. Although we did not examine existing circles for sex-offenders, we understand that early impressions are promising. There is no sign yet of sentencing circles but it is possible that they may be thought useful at some future point. We outline their use in Minnesota: they are resource intensive but have credibility and involve the community. Reparative boards in Vermont are staffed by community members, who agree the conditions of probation with offenders once orders have been made by courts. We did not specifically examine these in our report but, again, they are known to be popular and credible.

Q20:   What kind of judicial oversight of restorative justice is needed to ensure a reasonable consistency with sentencing practice and safeguard participants' human rights?

Judicial oversight is an essential aspect of mainstreaming. The New Zealand model, where the courts are used as a backstop, is often put forward as the best. Judges are concerned not only to ensure that agreements are reasonably appropriate but to monitor the quality of the process, accepting that this is differently conceived from court proceedings. Judicial training may be needed to raise awareness that it is the quality of the decision-making that is most important. Courts should be sure that agreements reflect negotiation and participation, that sufficient numbers have been present (in family group conferences) and that legal advice has been available beforehand.

In cases that are diverted from prosecution, participants will need to be clear that they may opt to go to court if they are unhappy at any stage about the fairness of the proceedings or agreement.

Q21: How far should information that emerges during a restorative process be inadmissible as evidence in court, so as to encourage the full participation of offenders and safeguard their human rights but without undermining the prosecution of offences?

Confidentiality is a difficult issue but the general principle is that information given by offenders in relation to the offence being mediated/conferenced is inadmissible as evidence in court. Information given by victims should always be confidential. There will be circumstances where concerns are raised that may prompt further investigations. In family mediation, child abuse is recognised to be one of these. Further consideration is necessary in the criminal justice context.

Q23: What are the particular needs of different sections of the community, such as women and members of ethnic minorities, to which restorative approaches need to be sensitive?

Ethnic minorities are in prison in disproportionate numbers and women offenders are being incarcerated at an increasing rate. Both demand pressing attention, part of which could be the offer of realistic alternatives. If these came by way of restorative interventions, they may well increase our understanding of needs that research has so far failed to achieve.

Our research showed that although restorative practice can be particularly helpful for women – as in custodial provision in Minnesota – it may also require special care. Difficult relationships are more likely to be the cause of women offending and while restorative work may help them to acknowledge this, they may also be too keen to accept responsibility. This may lead to overwhelming feelings of guilt and, in turn, to self-harm.

On the other hand, domestic violence mediation in Austria has helped women to feel more in control, even if it is no more successful than courts in reducing recidivism.

Q26: How far should provision of restorative justice, if integrated into the whole criminal justice system, be based on its current use in the youth justice system?

Restorative justice should be provided by means of an option at every stage of the criminal justice process. It will not always be appropriate but it must be available and flexible. In the case of a theft charge, for example, diversion may be the preferred course, but, in a murder case, the restorative intervention could be by way of a pre-sentence conference, to inform sentence planning for an inevitable prison sentence. We believe that the CPS should be given the power to divert, in line with Scotland, North America and other European countries. We do not preclude the extension of referral orders to adults but favour prosecutorial diversion.

Appendix 3 – Visits and meetings conducted by Shari Tickell for the project

United States

Minnesota

- Head and senior restorative justice planners from Department of Corrections Restorative Justice Initiative (DoC):
  - senior planners for female offenders;
  - roundtable discussion with practitioners from probation, juvenile probation, education, custodial facilities and community organisations, including the co-ordinators of the Washington County Court Service's Community Justice Program, the Woodbury Community Conferencing Program and the Hennepin County Juvenile Probation Dept.
- Attended the co-ordinating group for the Summit University/Frogtown Peacemaking Circle, which included Judge Wilson, the co-ordinator and two other members of the circle.
- Meeting with Professor Mark Umbreit from the University of Minnesota Center for Restorative Justice and Peacemaking.
- Meeting with the co-ordinator of the restorative conferencing project at Redwing custodial facility, and the opportunity to talk to some inmates.

Texas

- The founder and the current co-ordinator of the Victim Offender Mediation and Dialogue Program.
- Shown and watched a number of videos of mediations.
- The director of the victim witness division in Travis County (who, as a victim survivor, was also a key figure in the establishment of victims' services in Texas).
- The district attorney of Travis County, a keen proponent of restorative justice.

Austria

- Christa Pelikan from the University of Vienna, Department of Criminology.
- Roland Miklaus, Ministry of Justice.
- The head of the Vienna ATA (now part of the Neustart organisation).

- A mediation practitioner for the Vienna ATA.
- Judge Claudia Fenz from Vienna youth court and a senior prosecutor from the court.

Norway
- The senior policy advisor with responsibility for restorative justice within the Ministry of Justice.
- Professor Nils Christie from the University of Oslo University.
- A police officer and a prosecutor at Moss District police station.
- A probation manager.
- A mediation service co-ordinator.

Northern Ireland
- Brian White, Northern Ireland Office.
- Northern Ireland Association for the Care and Resettlement of Offenders.
- Kieran McEvoy from Queens University, Department of Law.
- The co-ordinators of Alternatives and Community Restorative Justice Ireland.

Scotland
- The director and four staff involved in policy and implementation of restorative justice initiatives.
- The Criminal Justice Director from the Scottish Executive.

England and Wales
- Managers or referral order co-ordinators at ten Youth Offending Teams (YOTs) or partnership agencies. YOTS in the north, south west and Wales were also consulted.
- Connect.
- The Bourne End restorative justice unit Thames Valley Police.
- The coordinator of the Justice research consortium in the London Crown Courts.